W0082888

IDENTITY, AUTHENTICITY, AND HUMILITY

The Aquinas Lecture, 2017

IDENTITY, AUTHENTICITY, AND HUMILITY

by

Daniel O. Dahlstrom

Under the auspices of the
Wisconsin-Alpha Chapter of Phi Sigma Tau

MARQUETTE
UNIVERSITY
PRESS

© 2017 Marquette University Press
Milwaukee, Wisconsin 53201-3141
All rights reserved.
www.marquette.edu/mupress/

Under the auspices of the
Wisconsin-Alpha Chapter of Phi Sigma Tau

LIBRARY OF CONGRESS CATALOGING-IN-PUBLICATION DATA

Names: Dahlstrom, Daniel O., author.
Title: Identity, authenticity, & humility / Daniel O. Dahlstrom.
Description: First [edition]. | Milwaukee : Marquette University
 Press, 2017.
 | Series: The Aquinas lecture ; No. 81, 2017 | Includes
bibliographical references.
Identifiers: LCCN 2016057842| ISBN 9780874621914
(hardcover : alk. paper) |
 ISBN 0874621917 (hardcover : alk. paper)
Subjects: LCSH: Self (Philosophy) | Identity (Philosophical
 concept) | Authenticity (Philosophy) | Humility.
Classification: LCC BD438.5 .D34 2017 | DDC 126—dc23
LC record available at https://urldefense.proofpoint.com/v2/
url?u=https-3A__lccn.loc.gov_2016057842&d=DwIFAg&c=
S1d2Gs1Y1NQV8Lx35_Qi5FnTH2uYWyh_OhOS94IqYCo
&r=hokKgJ4JxWGN8r507i6qR6wpZ-D_MmlVVO57591llH
Q&m=heVWwfXw51I5mY18nH2Iu7rfX1tCoicckuoPwjfx_
CE&s=GNoCtSyITGDU7Er6udb9o0bTWnEU2YtokSSZ
WrjDeNM&e=

♾ The paper used in this publication meets the minimum requirements of the American
National Standard for Information Sciences–
Permanence of Paper for Printed Library Materials, ANSI Z39.48-1992.

Association of American
University Presses

MARQUETTE UNIVERSITY PRESS
MILWAUKEE

The Association of Jesuit University Presses

PREFATORY

The Philosophy Department of Marquette University on behalf of Phi Sigma Tau, the Philosophy Honors Society, each year invites a scholar to deliver a lecture in honor of St. Thomas Aquinas.

Daniel O. Dahlstrom

The 2017 Aquinas Lecture, *Identity, Authenticity, and Humility*, was delivered on Sunday, February 26, 2017, by Dr. Daniel O. Dahlstrom, the John R. Silber Professor of Philosophy at Boston University. Dr. Dahlstrom served as Chair of the Boston University Department of Philosophy from 2007 to 2011.

Dr. Dahlstrom received his Ph.D. from St. Louis University in 1978. Before moving to Boston University he was a member of the School of Philosophy of The Catholic University of America from 1979 to 1996.

Midway between research as a Fulbright scholar at Tübingen (1974-75) and Bonn (1983-84) respectively, Dr. Dahlstrom received a grant from the Mellon Foundation for research on medieval logic at the Vatican Microfilm Library (1978). In 1986 a Humboldt award facilitated study of the theoretical works of Kant and Hegel at Cologne, and the Thyssen Foundation supported research on Heidegger in Freiburg in 2005 and 2013. He has also been a Visiting Professor at the Catholic University of Leuven and the University of Luxembourg.

In addition to producing translations of major works by Moses Mendelssohn, Friedrich Schiller, G. W. F. Hegel, Ludwig Feuerbach, Edmund Husserl, and Martin Heidegger, Dr. Dahlstrom has edited eighteen collections of essays, including *Interpreting Heidegger* in 2011. His books include *Das logische Vorurteil* (Passagen, 1994), *Heidegger's Concept of Truth* (Cambridge, 2001), *Philosophical Legacies* (CUA press, 2008), and *The Heidegger Dictionary* (Bloomsbury, 2013).

Numerous articles have appeared in such journals as *Review of Metaphysics, Research in Phenomenology, Kant-Studien, New Yearbook for Phenomenology and Phenomenological Philosophy, Reason Papers,*

Philosophical Forum, Idealistic Studies, Mind, The Thomist, Modern Schoolman, Techne, Philosophisches Jahrbuch, Jahrbuch für Recht und Ethik, and *British Journal of the History of Philosophy.* As a speaker, he has been much in demand, presenting numerous invited papers and keynote addresses at national and international conferences.

In addition to serving as president of both the Metaphysical Society of America and the American Catholic Philosophical Association, Dr. Dahlstrom was the first presiding officer of the Heidegger Circle of North America and, from 2010 to 2014, the first editor of its annual journal, *Gatherings.* He has directed over thirty doctoral dissertations and served as a reader on over forty dissertations, in his home department as well as in other departments, world-wide.

To Dr. Dahlstrom's distinguished list of publications, the Philosophy Department and Phi Sigma Tau are pleased to add: *Identity, Authenticity, and Humility.*

To

Joe, Mike, Pat, Bill, Bob, and Mary

ACKNOWLEDGMENTS

For helpful, critical readings of these lectures, I am grateful to Andrew Butler, Ian Dunkle, Lucas Fain, Joseph Gamache, Tobias Hoffmann, Walter Hopp, James Kinkaid, and Al and Maria Miller. Above all, Eugenie and Max have been endless sources of wonder and inspiration for the thoughts on these pages.

IDENTITY, AUTHENTICITY, AND HUMILITY

"This above all; to thine own self be true"
—*Hamlet*, Act 1, Scene 3, lines 78f

True enough, but how do I know that I am being true to myself or, for that matter, that being true to myself is an option? Even setting aside – perhaps all too peremptorily – the likelihood of hardened habits of self-deception, I am frequently mistaken about myself, deeming myself more courageous or less pretentious than I am. Nor, as the example of Hamlet instructs us, does one have to be of a particularly speculative mind to question what it means to be someone at all – though it may not hurt to be a little mad.

Mendacity is, of course, not the same as madness, fallibility, or ignorance. Dishonesty supposes a responsibility for myself that any of the latter can foreclose. Shakespeare's exhortation to authenticity assumes, in other words, some level of self-understanding and the potential to live up to it. By the same token, it assumes a difference between simply being ourselves and being true to ourselves, a difference in something like attenuations or levels of selfhood. This difference explains how we can be ourselves while failing to understand ourselves or live up to our potential to be our true selves. Nor is fallibility or ignorance a hindrance of the same magnitude as a malady. A person of sound mind can recognize her mistake or ignorance, but an illness can irremediably thwart self-understanding.

Complicating matters is the effect that an episode of being true or untrue to ourselves has on our self-understanding and vice versa. Self-understanding and being authentic are wound together like a double helix in constant motion, like the DNA of the individual life on which they supervene. On some levels, they are even indistinguishable; consider, for example, being who we are and understanding the language we grew up using. Yet, thanks to the understanding, we are also able, in certain situations, to take stock of ourselves.[1] Shakespeare's exhortation would seem to have traction only to the extent that self-understanding and being authentic, while distinct from one another, make common cause in a dynamic, iterated, yet ever-evolving process. In such a process, being ourselves (on one level) is necessary for understanding ourselves, and understanding ourselves is necessary for us to be true to ourselves (on another level, superseding the previous level).

There is, of course, no shortage of challenges to such an account of self-understanding and authen-

---

1   Understanding is then a kind of second intention, taking as its object a first intentional understanding, whether the latter be theoretical or practical, scientific or artistic, etc.

ticity, challenges that call into question the very plausibility of Shakespeare's exhortation to be true to ourselves. The following essay responds to three such challenges based respectively upon (1) the allegedly fragmentary character of our experiences, (2) ways that society shapes our personal identities, and (3) our fondness for others' esteem. We cannot be true to ourselves if there is no self, if our concept of ourselves is nothing more than a social construct, or if we let ourselves be defined by worries about others' regard for us. Challenges of the first sort are largely speculative, stemming from philosophical interpretations of the nature of human experience. Challenges of the second sort draw on ways that institutions, as social practices, form our personal identities. The third – and arguably primary – sort of challenge is existential, a matter of deciding to come face to face with ourselves despite what others might like us to be.

1. Speculative challenges

The challenges to self-understanding and authenticity presented by fallibility and ignorance merely scratch the surface of these challenges. Equally daunting is the sheer surfeit of characteristics that I and/or others rightly consider part of me. In addition to my memories, dreams, and aspirations, there are actions, omissions, physical qualities, and myriad relationships (intimate and private, mundane and public, social and political). In some cases it is my prerogative alone to recognize such characteristics; in other cases others are privy to them (we are blind, sometimes even incorrigibly, to characteristics that are obvious to friends and teachers, physicians and coaches).

These observations have two important implications. On the one hand, any measure of self-understanding and authenticity must be limited to characteristics that I have, or perhaps can have, self-consciously.[2] On the other hand, by the same token, my self-understanding is by no means all there is to my personal identity.

The immense variety of a person's characteristics at any time, including those beyond her purview at any moment, presents a natural challenge to a person's achievement of self-understanding. The unremitting transience of such characteristics presents a further challenge, indeed, in modern philosophy perhaps the central speculative challenge. This transience eliminates certain traditional conceptions of personal identity and, with it, the basis for any gen-

---

2   A self-conscious experience is an experience that includes awareness of having the experience, e.g., perceiving a tree with the awareness of doing so. Not all experiences, including conscious experiences, are self-conscious or, better, apperceptive in this sense; see my "Apperceptive and Non-Apperceptive Consciousness" in *Études Phénoménologiques / Phenomenological Studies*, Vol. 1 (forthcoming).

uine self-understanding. In the course of a lifetime (and even before and after it if we take others' anxious anticipations and fading memories of us into account), many characteristics simply disappear. Even those that persist change to some degree, sometimes drastically, adding to the complexity of who I might be. Fortune and misfortune, success and illness, conversion and loss punctuate the relentless before and after that make up a lifetime.

This transience famously led Hume to deny the plausibility of personal identity.[3] Devoid of personal identity, I can neither understand nor be true to myself. This sort of challenge is clearly speculative, since entertaining it, let alone accepting the force of it, requires a suspension of anything like leading an ordinary life. (Indeed, to return to Hamlet, it might require a moment of madness.) Hume himself – the champion of "common life" – appreciates this departure when, causing fits for his interpreters, he moves in his *Treatise* from the fictional self of speculation to the self of passion, "that identical person, of whose thoughts, actions and sensations we are intimately conscious."[4]

Framing the problem of personal identity along these lines, however, is hardly tied to Hume's par-

---

3   David Hume, *A Treatise of Human Nature*, L. A. Selby-Bigge and P. H. Nidditch (Oxford: Clarendon, 1978), 259: "The identity, which we ascribe to the mind of man, is only a fictitious one...."

4   Hume, *Treatise*, 329, 339.

ticular cognitive model of discrete, momentary perceptions. Even as the details of that model are discredited, the dilemma persists in the form of metaphysical perdurantism, i.e., the view that nothing persists (extreme or eliminative perdurantism) or that, if something persists, it is not fundamental but reducible to facts involving only instantaneous things, e.g., time-slices or person-stages (reductive perdurantism).[5] Personal identity as an ontological identity over time typically gives way today to a form of physical continuity or, more frequently, psychological continuity.[6]

But, even if one contests – as I do below – assumptions underlying this challenge to the persistence of selfhood and the ensuing project of re-identification, a person's movements through time and space, individually and interpersonally, continue to present familiar, natural problems for self-understanding. Age, health, relationships, accomplishments and setbacks, changing environments are just some of the factors

---

5   Derek Parfit, *Reasons and Persons* (Oxford: Clarendon, 1984); Sydney Shoemaker, "A Materialist's Account" in *Personal Identity*, ed. Shoemaker and Richard Swinburne (Oxford: Blackwell, 1984); Robert C. Koons and Timothy H. Pickavance, *Metaphysics: The Fundamentals* (Oxford: Wiley Blackwell, 2015), 212.

6   See Marya Schechtman, *The Constitution of Selves* (Ithaca: Cornell University Press, 1996), 13-25; Eric T. Olson, "Personal Identity" in *Stanford Encyclopedia of Philosophy* (2015).

that have an effect on an ever-developing self-perception. Moreover, each of these factors may have its particular effect to different degrees at different intervals. Hence, we need to grapple with the notion of something like attenuations of selfhood. For example, insofar as someone does not initiate all her movements, it would seem that the movements that she does, did, or will initiate are somehow more hers than those that are not.[7] Above all, while what she is at any juncture is inseparable from what she has been and aspires to be, she remains unfinished, subject to the inscrutableness of what is to come. In this respect at least, she is – and must remain – a mystery to herself.

***

Fair enough, one might respond, but neither that mystery nor the surfeit of characteristics flagged above rule out the possibility of a measure of self-understanding sufficient to abide by the exhortation to authenticity. After all, as noted above, self-understanding is one thing, personal identity quite another. Moreover, as the talk of attenuation suggests, the characteristics that I associate with myself are not all on the same level; nor presumably are those that others associate with me. Some are salient, i.e., patently

---

7   Someone is accountable if a series of events can be traced to something she has done; she is responsible if she performed the action deliberately.

more important than other characteristics at any given time and over time. I was born in Wisconsin, but I don't think that this property defines me; others may think otherwise.

What is arguably far more important than any passing sentiment or nonchalant remark are characteristics that make up a person's character. We customarily identify people on the basis of regular, relatively constant ways of behaving; i.e., they are variously irascible, dedicated, athletic, and so on. These character-defining ways of behaving form an important part of their respective personal identities.[8] Someone who understands herself in terms of any of these salient characteristics may be said to have a discriminating self-understanding.

Although a person cannot know with any certainty what will become of her while in possession of the salient characteristics, past experience of them or their ilk provides, at least within certain parameters,

---

8   Some of these ways of behaving make up a person's *moral* character, the enduring patterns of behavior for which she is responsible, e.g., her fidelity or infidelity. Thus, we speak of a "villainous character" and, more honorifically, of someone having character (usually meaning a "virtuous" character). Glossing Mill's treatment, James describes character as "an aggregate of tendencies to act in a firm and prompt and definite way upon all principal emergences of life"; William James, *Principles of Psychology*, Volume One (New York: Holt, 1890), 125. James also places 'characters' in apposition to 'selves,' as possibilities that are chosen (ibid., 310; see, too, ibid., 288).

a reliable guide to her prospects, not least her prospects of being true to herself. In other words, she can only be true to herself if she understands herself in terms of who she truly is, i.e., in terms of salient characteristics of her personal identity. Demonstrating the saliency of certain characteristics for self-understanding is undoubtedly a tall order. Yet that demonstration is not, *prima facie*, an insuperable task, especially since so much of experience points to a substantial, albeit unfinished identity underlying those characteristics.

Reflexive memories, for example, in addition to being crucial to any self-understanding, point to an identity of this sort.[9] It is one thing for someone to remember an oak tree, another to remember seeing an oak tree. The former is a case of non-reflexive memory, the latter of reflexive memory. In the latter case, the remembering and what is remembered coincide; there is some indexical marker that applies identically to the person remembering and the person who saw the oak true.[10]

---

9   Thomas Reid, *Essays on the Intellectual Powers of Man* (Edinburgh: Bell, 1785), 316: "Identity in general, I take to be a relation between a thing that is known to exist at one time, and a thing which is known to have existed at another time." Ibid., 319: "...it is not my remembering any action of mine that makes me to be the person who did it."

10   The warrant for this sameness is limited to the experience of reflexive memory itself, an experience more akin to perceiving than to believing. Whereas beliefs can

Explicit, reflexive memories are commonplace and fallible, but generally reliable (as success of reliance upon them attests). Remembering that we had a certain experience is worlds apart from imagining that we did. Such memories are unquestionably our access – in a certain respect, our only access – to our past as ours. This access to the past as ours is crucial to self-understanding, disclosing as it does that the remembering and the remembered are in some vital respect the same. We make promises and contracts; we confess our sins and judge our motives; we harbor grievances and forgive perceived insults – in each case while remembering our previous states of mind (even where we project their continued or discontinued efficacy), remembering and thus understanding them *as ours*. Note, too, that, these states of mind are often available in public settings that supply authenticating criteria. Questions of guilt and innocence in a courtroom turn on the application of such criteria. Signatures on contracts, affidavits, and deeds provide patent examples of public evidence for a person's past actions and states of mind.

---

be warranted by what is believed (apart from my act of believing them), my act of remembering myself seeing, believing, etc. is often all the evidence available for doing so. A reflexive memory is a person's memory of herself or her actions as the same person, not a belief about that sameness. Nor can this sameness, strictly speaking, be that of a copy to an original, since the original no longer exists.

Less patent (at least publicly) but no less efficacious are internal markers of past actions and states of mind, such as certain memories' painfulness (a society's means of insuring, Nietzsche stresses, that they are not forgotten). As time passes, some memories can become less vivid and more ambiguous, and yet, while ever fallible, they can be veracious. While an adult's memory of a frightening experience pales in comparison with the childhood experience, the memory and its credibility endure.

A person's reflexive memory is, as noted, a memory of a past experience as hers, where the personal pronoun 'her' refers in her mind to the same person who is remembering the experience. Reflexive memory thus supposes *her* having this or that experience. So, too, if she believes that she saw the oak tree, it is typically because she remembers doing so, and such a belief is reliably true because memories are. So, too, when veracious, a reflexive memory entails that identity, not merely the supposition or belief in it. Yet just as a memory is not true by virtue of being reflexive, so her personal identity (her self, who she is) is not created simply by her memories. Nor does forgetting a past experience that can be correctly attributed to me eliminate the identity involved.[11]

---

11   The brave officer who forgets having been flogged is still the very person who was flogged, as Reid notes in making his case against the Lockean view that memory constitutes identity (ibid., 333-34).

***

Yet, if reflexive memories suppose but do not themselves constitute or make-up the personal identity in question, what is the status of the identity? How are we to understand the personal identity that is supposed by reflexive memories? One possible answer lies in the nature of the experiences remembered. I remember looking for poison ivy in order to avoid it, running my hand over a sanded surface to test its smoothness, and passing on the habaneros offered at a particular restaurant. In each case an aim is a non-negotiable part of the experience,[12] as is some corporeal dimension that involves my body and its own organic identity. Closer consideration of these experiences provides a key aspect of self-understanding and reason for contesting Hume's skepticism regarding personal identity. In order to make this point, however, I need to address first the relevant notion of identity.

Let us start from the premise that everything in nature is in motion, changing relentlessly, albeit each

---

12   To be sure, not all experiences are experienced as purposively recursive. *Prima facie* at least, aesthetic experiences are arguably not purposive experiences and, like some acts of theorizing, their content is not determined by how they supervene on sub-personal processes that make up a person's organic identity. So, too, there is reason to think that the embodied character of these experiences (proving a theorem, writing a novel) will differ markedly from those that are purposively recursive.

at different tempos and in different ways. Nature itself changes, but it does so – at least for long periods – in a more or less stable manner. Within nature, different sorts of changes correspond to different degrees of stability (persistence and self-sustainment), dependent, to a large degree, on the respective environment. Weather patterns, waves, and winds come and go; they are inherently transient and short-lived. By contrast, an animal organism, if its environment co-operates, maintains itself by carrying out a specific set of interrelated functions for a time. It is a stable unity of specifically coordinated functions, designed to keep it afloat in a sea of opportunities and threats. Organisms, too, pass away like the wind, but before they do, they persist by initiating and reacting to changes. Nourishing and protecting itself (and detecting things accordingly in its environment) exemplify these sorts of changes *in* and *to* the organism. The emergence and demise of the entire organism obviously make up a radically different sort of change.

Every change, it would seem, has extrinsic and intrinsic identities (diachronic unities), made up of properties it possesses in relation to changes external and internal to it respectively, e.g., changes in its surroundings and changes in its make-up. Different sorts of change and corresponding identities mark events and organisms respectively. What distinguishes a mere event (like yesterday's weather) from an organism is the organism's hand in maintaining itself throughout changes that it undergoes and/or initiates. Its intrinsic identity is, in other words, a more or less persisting, self-maintained identity.[13]

In nature, it bears iterating, there is no identity without pertinent differences (being in different states, being at different intervals, interacting with different things).[14] The differences in question are essential to an organism's intrinsic identity. Change in general requires a transition from being one way one time to being another way another time or to not being at all. An organic identity corresponds to the former sort of change. It persists by actively re-

---

13   An organism has a 'self-maintained identity' insofar as its functions are purposefully related to one another (diachronically and synchronically) for the sake of that organism as a whole. In animal organisms, the phenomenal character of conscious experiences appears to reflect their embeddedness in these purposeful, combined functions of reacting and initiating actions. Consciously experiencing and explicitly maintaining such identity is a distinctively human marker. This identity, it bears iterating, is not separate from the changes enacted and undergone by the organism, i.e., it is not something absolutely identical from time to time.

14   The notion that a difference is inherent in any real identity may reveal a source of Hume's confusion about personal identity. Once identity is confined to a putatively timeless relation of ideas, removed from any change, it is obviously hopeless, indeed, downright confused to look for it in matters of fact, such as the fact of organic change.

lating to itself in the sense of being (changing) "for the sake of itself."

Another way to put this last point is to note that, as long as an organism survives, what distinguishes changes peculiar to it from other changes in nature is an identity that it has by sustaining and stabilizing itself in constant interaction with its environment. It reaches out to the environment in a purposively recursive (reflexive) manner for the sake of – at a minimum – maintaining itself. The organism exists only to the extent that it maintains this identity by carrying out certain co-ordinated functions (such as, for example, nourishment and repair). The organism performs these self-serving functions by reaching out, temporally and spatially at once, to its environment. Yet, despite their differences, these functions belong to the same organic identity.

While specific, an animal organism is also in each case unique, with its own distinctive emergence (birth) and genetic make-up, its no less unique, inherited and persisting traits and experiences.[15]

---

15   Although each of us has a unique DNA structure, thinking through its relation to the conception of "my body" is daunting; see Michael Allen Fox, "A New Look at Personal Identity" in *Philosophy Now* (online journal): "It also turns out that only ten percent of the DNA present within our bodies belongs to our own cells; the rest resides within the ten to one hundred trillion bacteria and other organisms of several hundred species which inhabit our bodies....My body is no longer simply *my* body."

The way in which an organic identity continuously maintains itself is largely structural and functional, recognizable by virtue of similarities across differences, whether they be initiated internally and/or externally. Such an organism's stability is, in metaphysical parlance, that of a unique, *enduring* identity, maintaining itself as a stratified whole as it reaches out to its surroundings.[16] An identity of this sort is not a timeless identity corresponding to some sort of mathematical idea. While it can be considered in abstraction from different behaviors and properties at different times, this identity and those differences are really inseparable from one another. The organism's identity cannot be adequately described without invoking its differences over time and vice versa.

As is the case for any animal organism, most of the self-stabilizing functions of a human being's organic identity (and thereby her personal identity) lie below the threshold of experience and self-understanding. When they are experienced, they often depend upon how it reaches out to the external world. Familiar markers, again both within and without, make it clear that there is something of the reality of a person's present experiences that is the same as

---

16   This sort of functional identity suggests an Aristotelian response to Theseus-ship types of objections, given that a human body's material make-up over a certain period is completely different. For a valuable discussion, see John Bowin, "Aristotle on Identity and Persistence," *Apeiron* 41/1 (March 2008): 65-88.

the reality of her past experiences. It is in terms of these ways of being present to ourselves individually and presenting ourselves to the surrounding world and others collectively that our personal identities are grounded in our organic identities, i.e., our living bodies (though those identities by no means begin and end there). This is obvious in the case of a person's public or social identity. A person's voice, for example, can be a dead give-away; a photo on a driver's license is a means of identification. DNA analysis is in a certain respect the gold standard of identification, revealing as it does both specific and unique markers of an organic identity's intrinsic code — and giving a new meaning to the notion of "family resemblance."

At the same time, the purposively recursive character of organic identity (self-maintaining, self-stabilizing, self-nourishing, and so on) is experienced itself, in concert with the ways the organism reaches out to its surroundings. The feedback is experiential; I experience performing basic functions as being for me, for the organism that I am. To use broad neurophysiological terms, different kinds of experiences — interoceptive, exteroceptive, kinaesthetic and proprioceptive — supervene on the living, human organism and the neural networks vital to its organic identity.[17] These experiences are directly grounded in the

---

17   Charles Sherrington, *The Integrative Action of the Nervous System* (New Haven: Yale University Press, 1906), 256, 324; and my "Interoception and Self-awareness:

body's position, functions, movements, etc., within a specific environment for the sake of the human organism as a whole. What is more, they are frequently experienced as such. From the experience of the iteration of one or more of these kinds of experiences, involving the most elementary sort of memory and recognition of similarities, a rudimentary sense of the ordered unity of these functions emerges and, with it, evidence of the body's organic identity. (An infant begins to remember, i.e., to detect the familiarity of kinaesthetic experiences of moving her leg, of interoceptive experiences of hunger and thirst, of exteroceptive experiences of her mother's caresses.[18]) This sense of a functional, purposive unity grows, not only with each iteration and recognition of the same, but also with the interaction and coordination of these experiences and the eventual recognition of those interactions and co-ordinations.

An Exploration in Interoceptive Phenomenology" in *Philosophy of Mind and Phenomenology*, ed. D. O. Dahlstrom, Andreas Elpidorou, and Walter Hopp (New York: Routledge, 2015), 141-164.

18   Similarly, a person experiences a headache "in" her head (interoceptively) as the same sort of ache she experienced yesterday; so, too, because she's done something like this before, she reaches out (kinaesthetically) to the cold beer she sees (exteroceptively) on the table, anticipating and already relishing (affectively) the taste of it.

With developments of this sort in mind, neuro-physiologists speak of an "integrative system," comprising the "material me."[19] Sometimes taken for granted in these discussions is what I am calling the organism's 'purposively recursive outreach,' echoing Aristotle's account of τὸ οὗ ἕνεκα causation (*Physics* 194b33). Always in motion, i.e., always in some complex state of acting and reacting to something at a particular place and time, a person's organic identity is the ever-developing center of gravity of these functions. To the extent that I experience these functions as such, I experience myself or at least my "material me" as their unifying purpose. I eat because I am hungry, I flinch because I sense a threat, I move closer to someone so that I may hear them, I avert my eyes from the sun to protect myself from its glare, I scratch an itch in the hope of alleviating it. In each instance, the experience is purposive, "for me" – and no one else.[20]

---

19   T. E. Feinberg, *From Axons to Identity: Neurological Exploration of the Nature of the Self* (New York: Norton, 2009); Antonio Damasio, *Self Comes to Mind: Constructing the Conscious Brain* (New York: Vintage, 2012).

20   On the distinctive 'for me-like' character of experiences, see note 40. An exclusively mechanical account of experiences, where experiences of a certain sort cause experiences of another sort, can only succeed if the experiences of the respective sorts are describable independently from one another. But the purposively recursive character of experiences flagged above rules

Countless experiences of this sort of purposively recursive outreach are readily demonstrable. The content of such experiences directly contradicts presumptions that my experiences are inherently disjointed or that they can be adequately characterized in isolation from interactions with surroundings (there is no outreach without something to reach out to). Modern eliminative approaches to personal identity make these presumptions. They suppose an account of experiences that abstracts from how they supervene *experientially* on an organic identity interacting with its surroundings. That is to say, they simply omit or turn a blind eye to a fundamental component of these experiences, namely, the ways they are experienced as part of my body's vital functions, as being for its (my) own sake. To be sure, a person's organic identity does not coincide with the unitary flow of her experiences or her self-understanding as it emerges from those experiences. In addition to falling under quite different descriptions (e.g., an MRI of a muscle tear as opposed to the feel of it), the intermittent character of those experiences contrasts with the organism's constant striving for homeostasis. Yet, if the foregoing account of the character of human experiences is correct, the practice of portraying them as discrete perceptions or time-slices – the core of eliminativist approaches – misrepresents them fundamentally. That is to say, it ignores how

---

out this independence. The thirst that motivates me to drink is not thirst simply but *my* thirst.

they are united for the most part in purposively ordered ways that serve to maintain and, if possible,
enhance the organic identity of the person having
the experiences.[21]

When I stated earlier that so much of experience
points to a substantial, unfinished identity, part of
what I had in mind is not only experience's grounding in the organic identities of our bodies, but also
the considerable extent to which that grounding is
integral to the experience. In short, our experiences are embodied experiences – and experienced as
such. This experiential grounding in our body's organic identity is, in effect, an experience of a kind of
supervenience.[22] While by no means the same as the
function involved, this sort of experience frequently
meshes with that function. This experience of supervenience is patent in experiences that are directly
corporeal, from experiences largely centered in a single organ (e.g., seeing, hearing, headaches) to those
more broadly coordinated among multiple organs

---

21   "For the most part" is a necessary qualifier here, given
self-destructive behavior, but it may not be sufficient
to explain the latter's pervasiveness if, as argued here,
there is a basic unity between the purposive character
of experience and the process of maintaining/enhancing
an organic identity. But responding to this considerable
challenge must be reserved for another day.

22   Victor Caston, "Aristotle and supervenience," *The
Southern Journal of Philosophy* XXXI, supplement
(1993): 107-35.

(e.g., breathing, walking). But it is no less apparent, upon reflection, in experiences that are not immediately corporeal in the same way (e.g., reading, typing, playing). As a person lives through these experiences, she experiences them as embodied, even if the corporeality of a particular experience takes a backseat to its main import. Thus, only in passing does a person bringing in the groceries feel the weight of the bags in her arms; late for an appointment in rush hour, she barely feels the contours of the steering wheel in her grasp; she only remotely senses her fingers striking keys as she types.[23]

Given the routineness and routinely purposive necessity of these functions, coupled with the intimacy of our identification with our bodies reaching out in terms of them, we typically need to stop and reflect, interrupting those routines, to see how our experiences embody these functions. Yet concerted reflection is not necessary to appreciate this point; illness and breakdowns often do the job for us. When fatigue or pain set in, when something goes awry in

23   Even experiences that seem paradigmatically passive – like perceptions (the experience favored by modern eliminativists) – supervene on our bodies in ways that illustrate the experiences' active and embodied dimension. In perception, we experience things and not merely the profiles afforded by them, because we project, as part of the experience, a matrix of possible corporeal movements. The perception of unitary objects depends, in short, upon the intrinsic unity of perceptual experience and our sense of embodied possibilities.

in our bodies, and/or physical obstacles prove to be too much, the embodied character of our experience moves to center stage, sometimes with an alarming and ferocious alacrity (think of the onset of vertigo, a heart attack, rupture of an Achilles tendon).

Each of these experiences is, on one level, describable as a purely physical event. Such descriptions hold because human experiences are invariably embedded in an anatomical and physiological matrix of processes and activities proper to a living human body. A trenchant analysis of human experience – not least personal, self-conscious experiences – cannot fail to take into account its embeddedness in this matrix.

***

In the past few paragraphs I have been trying to make the case for the extent to which we experience, quite self-consciously, the purposively recursive outreach that marks our respective body's organic identity. When I drink because I am thirsty, this recursive activity is one that supervenes on a sub-personal process of self-maintenance, aiming at homeostasis. It is precisely this sort of experience of myself, my material me, not only in drinking but drinking for my sake (the sake of my organic identity) that provides a robust experiential basis for the identity supposed by reflexive memories and, by extension, self-understanding. As a purposively recursive experience of reaching out, the experience of drinking because *I* am thirsty (and thus for my sake) is an experience of myself – albeit a self, to be sure, that, like my organic identity, is nothing static, nothing independent of the differences and the interactions that mark the changes distinctive of it. In light of these sorts of experiences that are fundamental to whatever else we are, modern misgivings about personal identity – and any threat they may present to Shakespeare's exhortation – appear ill-founded if not confused (e.g., applying a conception of logical or mathematical identity to an identity that supposes change, as part of its extrinsic and intrinsic identity).

Such misgivings trade on diluted and fragmented views of experience, abstracting from what Brentano labels their "kinship" (think of the kinship of thirst and drinking).[24] Drawing on Brentano, William James makes an analogous point, when he faults the modern tradition for failing to see that while conscious states may be discrete and denumerable, their contents flow into one another with overlapping densities and effects.[25] James famously describes

---

24   Franz Brentano, *Psychologie vom empirischen Standpunkt*, Band I (Leipzig: Dunker & Humblot, 1874), 219.

25   James, *Principles of Psychology*, 240: "Into the awareness of the thunder itself the awareness of the previous silence creeps and continues; what we hear when the thunder crashes is not thunder *pure* but thunder-breaking-upon-silence-and-contrasting-with-it."

consciousness as a stream or "an alternation of flights and perchings,"[26] the contents of which are not punctuated by some indifferent third party's ordinal denumeration of states of consciousness (1st, 2nd, 3rd, etc.). Along with the tendency to disjoin the contents of experience from one another in this way, modern thinkers take over from Galileo and Descartes an analogous tendency to treat the givens of experience as separate qualities (e.g., primary, secondary, tertiary) at the expense of its syn-aesthetic and sym-pathetic richness.[27] As James puts it, "the 'simple impression' of Hume, the 'simple idea' of Locke are both abstractions, never realized in experience."[28]

The modern proclivity of considering psychological states (the mind) in abstraction from the life (organic identity) and life experiences that inform them may be a holdover of Descartes' twin insights that

---

26 James, *Principles of Psychology*, 243.

27 'Syn-aesthetic richness' stands for the ways that sensations resonate with one another; 'sym-pathetic richness' for their affective qualities and resonances. The softness, like the harshness, of a color bleeds into similar qualities of sounds and touches, all the while charged with an emotive import that comes with life's activities, projects, and fragility. So, too, we hear not decibels of sound pressure levels but a baby's cries to be comforted; we pick a flat stone that will skip across the river's surface; we feel not simply the icy path's slippery touch but also the danger it presents.

28 James, *Principles of Psychology*, 487.

our access to our own experiences is as close as we get to a sure thing and that those experiences themselves are not geometric, at least not in the way bodies are for a Cartesian (the idea of length is not long). Yet everything turns on unpacking the character of those experiences as such, holding at bay assumptions – not least, assumptions about bodies – that the experiences themselves do not call for. (Just as the contents of consciousness are not discontinuous, so they are not dis-embodied, though Cartesian geometry is ill-suited to capture their corporeality.)

The tendency to sever conscious experiences and their contents from the embodied life on which they depend is also betrayed by the ease with which some thinkers employ the image of a "theatre" (a "tablet," a "storehouse," a "computer") as a metaphor for the mind or the self.[29] (One hears echoes of the theater image in subsequent uses of narrative.) These metaphors limp, but not, as Hume suggests, because they misleadingly suggest something static. Instead these metaphors mislead by intimating that the make-up of the mind or self is, at bottom, no different from that of some artifact that we can devise and then master or control.

Our lives are not artifacts and what control we have over them is limited. Grounded in the organic identity of a natural substance that maintains itself over time – enduring rather than perduring, in contemporary jargon – a human life is necessarily

29   Hume, *Treatise*, 253.

self-stabilizing in certain respects. But, far from being self-sufficient, this self-stabilizing takes place, as it does for any animal organism, through a process of constantly reaching out to its environment and interacting with it both pre-experientially and experientially. Depending upon the environment and the organism's genetic make-up, the interaction not only sustains the organism but allows it to flourish – albeit always only to a degree and for a time. Life experiences, whether they be ours or those of other animals, are grounded in a fundamental set of capacities, functions, and relations.[30] Like the life of any animal, a human being's life experiences have stages, always informed by desires and fears that prompt a continual engagement with things and others for one sake or another, while issuing in accompanying pleasures and pains.

***

Throughout all the forms of outreach to things and others in the environment that are part of a person's organic identity, perceptions play a paramount role. As a lived experience, supervening on the processes of sustaining a life, perception is anything but randomly episodic. Although it presupposes the presence of what is perceived (a presence that, in contrast to phantasies, it does not fabricate), perception

---

30   Many of these functions must be sustained as a matter of life and death (when the organic identity is "finished").

plays its role in life experiences by being selective and meaningful. In other words, perceptions are inherently interpretive; they are perceptions of things and others *as* such-and-such. In this regard they are inseparable from memories and anticipations, guided (ultimately if not proximately) by desire (ὄρεξις); interpretations that steer perceptions are, as it were, at the intersection of such memories and anticipations.[31]

At this intersection, a person can also dwell on possible interpretations in the form of images and thoughts, a process that leads to the immense power of rationality (where the capacity to compare and contrast what is thought as such takes center stage). Thinking is interpretation temporarily suspended from its native task of informing a perception, but with an eye to it. None of these features at work in interpretations – memories and anticipations, images and thoughts, desires and reasons – are to be con-

---

31   Perception, as I construe it, is not the same as sensation nor does it even coincide necessarily with sensation, though sensory perception is a paradigmatic form of perception. Just as we perceive things within our visual fields or, more typically, across sensory fields, so, too, we perceive situations, states of affairs, relationships, times and places, possibilities, abstract entities, recurrent structures, and what is generally essential. But we also (and no less fundamentally) perceive what to do and how to do it, what things are for and how to use them. So, too, we use tools and wield implements perceptively (and not less fundamentally than we perceive things or situations).

fused with perceptions. Though one or more of them has a hand in guiding perceptions, none of them can replace perception. Even rationality, in comparing and contrasting what is thought as such with a view to interpreting what is perceptible, takes its cues from perception. Perception has this privileged status because it is only in perceptions that things, others, events, situations, implements, objectives, surroundings, etc. become apparent to us, whether tacitly or explicitly. As our sole access to these things as such, perceptions are essential to understanding the world in which we live and have an identity.

The interpretive dimension of perceptions highlighted here – rooted in but not reducible to the purposively recursive outreach of life and life experiences discussed above – is obviously limited in certain respects. Appearances can be deceiving, something crucial can be hidden from us. The interpretive dimension (again, at the intersection of memory and anticipation, potentially coinciding with imagining and thinking) is nonetheless what enables the perceiver to see the world as one thing or another and, in some cases, as it is. (Kant has, to be sure, a different set of concerns, but he nonetheless makes a similar point when he notes the blindness of intuitions without concepts and the emptiness of intuition-less thoughts.) Thus, the interpretive character of perception makes possible the arguably most important kind of perception: a true or veracious perception.

The importance of this kind of perception is patent: without the prospect of it, Shakespeare's exhortation would again ring hollow – this time not from lack of a plausible conception of the self or self-understanding but from a deficit of truth. A person's perceptions are *veracious* when what-she-perceives-(interprets)-things-as is what-they-are. A person is *cognizant* when she knows that her interpretations coincide with true perceptions or, in the absence of coincidence, that they would coincide, were what is perceived to present itself and the perception of it to take place. In this sense, true perceptions are vital for what I am here calling our 'cognizance' of things, others, practices, situations, and, not least, ourselves.

Although cognizance supposes true perceptions, it crucially supplements them with an awareness of perceiving something as it is. The awareness that counts for cognizance is existential and first personal in the sense that no one else can do it for us. In order for a person to be cognizant, it is necessary for her to be aware that she is perceiving something as it is.[32] In other words, to be cognizant of something is to be self-consciously aware of what it truly is. Cognizance of ourselves is, accordingly, being self-con-

---

32   Cognizance thus supposes some rudimentary form of apperception (self-consciousness). While analogues to apperception can be found in other experiences, it is one thing to remember remembering, another thing to do so self-consciously, yet another to be cognizant of the fact.

sciously aware of who we truly are, perceiving ourselves as such.

Cognizance, like other sorts of experience or forms of consciousness, has a primitive dimension to it that is irreducible to those other experiences or forms of consciousness. This primitive character, however, does not prevent us from distinguishing cognizance of something from merely thinking or perceiving, imagining or dreaming it. The fact that these experiences are part of the object in our cognizance of ourselves complicates matters, to be sure. Nevertheless, it remains the case that we are cognizant of ourselves to the extent that we are aware of perceiving ourselves and our experiences for what they are, i.e., aware that how we think of ourselves coincides with our self-perception.

As described above, perceptions in general – and, by extension, cognizance or understanding – are not strictly binary operations. Particular temporal-spatial, more or less moving contexts (environments, horizons) both enable and limit perceptions. Each perception ignores or neglects parts of the context and only partially or implicitly interprets other parts, as it fixes its attention on what is necessary for the purposes at hand. Experience is replete, in other words, with tacit features, components that are peripheral or tangential to what perception targets.

The contextual (horizonal) character is exceedingly complex, working on synchronic and diachronic levels at once. Attention to something in the foreground, for example, comes synchronically at the expense of the background. The diachronic level is perhaps more obvious in examples that highlight the joint movement of the experience and what is experienced. (I am running to catch the ball in flight; I swerve to avoid the passing traffic.) Just as the background is necessary to the Gestalt of what is foregrounded, so the where-from and where-to are necessary to its foregroundedness *now*. Despite its complexity, this diachronic character expresses the rudimentary structure of the interpretations that, building on memories and anticipations, steer perceptions.

The parallel just drawn with interpretation underscores the at once limiting and enabling character of contexts. On the one hand, the partiality of perception, due to contextual limitations, rules out a full disclosure of reality (if it is possible, indeed, to give a coherent meaning to that notion). In Leibnizian-Husserlian terminology, human perception can be accurate (true), but it is never fully adequate, capable of explicitly taking in all that bears upon it. The partiality of perception, moreover, is not due simply to the limitations of our powers of perception or the fact that we are only interested in a part of the world. The world always presents itself to us only partially. As Heraclitus tells us, nature invariably manages to do what it loves, i.e., to hide. As a result, self-understanding is inherently limited and so then, too, is our capacity to be authentic. On the other hand, it is precisely the where-to of experience, rooted in shared biologies and histories, inseparable from a corresponding where-from, that makes perception possible. Indeed, both self-preservation and any degree of flourishing depend upon this dynamic. Without the particular synthesis of memories and anticipations that gives rise to our interpretations, we would be lost in our worlds – and utterly unable to be true to ourselves.

A full complement of pursuits and passions – leisurely and labor-intensive, utilitarian and contemplative, routine and celebratory, artistic and technological, industrial and scientific – lives from perceptions in all the senses flagged above (interpretive, veracious, and partial) and from the understanding and cognizance produced by them. These perceptions and cognizance are never independent of particular horizons or context. To the extent that we engage in these pursuits and passions, we obviously can only understand and be true to ourselves in terms of them.

***

Modern philosophers rightly recognized that the possibility of self-understanding turns on a careful consideration of the character of our experience. I have been trying to impress upon you that our experiences are best understood as life experiences, both in the sense that those experiences are grounded in being alive and in the sense that this grounding is to a large degree quite palpable, indeed, making up a crucial part of the character of experience. The kinship and indelible richness of experiences, flagged above, is due precisely to this crucial dimension of being embedded in activities of living with their distinctive temporal-spatial horizons. Yet this crucial dimension, if not missing, is underappreciated in many modern approaches.

The reference to 'temporal-spatial' horizons above is an attempt to ward off the tendency of construing these aspects of experience in terms of space-time, i.e., in purely dimensional, geometrical – albeit non-Euclidean – terms. Anticipating is a key source of our fundamental experience of time; reaching out to things or others (in view of anticipating some transaction with them) provides us with our first inkling of space. In such a time-space, something is always at stake, there is always something to be decided.[33] Experience's embeddedness in these temporal-spatial horizons gives rise to its pervasively affective and rhythmic texture. Just as there is a necessary rhythm to a living organism's functions as it reaches out prospectively to its environs, so life experiences have their own rhythms, as we reach out, prospectively, to things and others. A prospective outreach brings with it, moreover, its own affective character.

---

33   Time-space is the field of decision and, hence, not purely dimensional.

The term 'prospective' here is meant to underscore the future-oriented, unfinished, and purposive character of the process. Our prospects are the indexical confluence of the personal biology and social history that make up, more concretely, our respective time-space. Thanks to this confluence, we project possibilities – we are always "ahead of ourselves" – for the sake of one thing or another in light of what we take to be at stake. In keeping with the nature of this confluence, our outreach and, with it, our selves are respectively unfinished (still alive!). These projections give rise at once to two features highlighted earlier, namely, the interpretations that permeate our perceptions and the emotional accents of our experiences.

To be sure, experiences, so construed, require that we are able to recognize recurring tokens of types as promising or threatening and to repeat patterns of behaving accordingly. The substantial identity of a living body – including, above all, what is at stake for it – requires the ability and motivation to detect and negotiate these types of things in our environment. Relying on those recurrences and these motivated abilities, human desires and fears make common cause with memories and anticipations in projecting certain results and acting on those projections. These projections and accompanying actions (the stuff of my experiences) move in concert with the way my body lives and flourishes by orienting its positions and movements. The term 'concert' here is meant to signify not simply an isomorphism or even a congruency, but the affective and rhythmic texture of experiences.

What accounts for the human body's basic stability is a structural and functional identity that permeates our experiences, giving them their rhythmic texture. Hume is right: there is no perception or mental quality that is numerically identical across time. But he is wrong to look for the basis of personal identity in an isolated perception, not only because there are, strictly speaking, no such perceptions, but more importantly because I have a personal, open-ended history that is grounded in the living, organic identity of my body. Personal identity is accordingly not so much a given, as Hume's inquiry seems to suppose it would have to be, as it is a ongoing prospect of what it means to be alive, always already reaching out to things and others in a purposively recursive way with a permanently fraught, affective and rhythmic texture of its own.

***

In addition to the challenges to authenticity that spring from the transience of experience, there are two further speculative challenges that deserve to be addressed. These traditional challenges are aimed at the prospect of self-understanding insofar as it is construed as a form of self-consciousness. As noted more than once, the field of self-understanding and authenticity does not comprise all the characteristics that are or can be attributed to me; it includes instead all and only the characteristics that I have or can have self-consciously. There can be no question of being honest with ourselves about characteristics of which we are not, or cannot be made, conscious.

Philosophers have repeatedly challenged the notion of self-consciousness, however, on the grounds that it engenders an infinite regress or that consciousness in general escapes our grasp. The former challenge assumes that the consciousness of which one is conscious is cut off from the act of being conscious of it, with obviously disastrous consequences for self-consciousness. On this assumption, in any putative consciousness of consciousness, the former is a subject, the latter an object. But, then, consciousness plays an endless game of catch-up with itself, never able to be aware of itself just as it is.[34] In an effort to preserve the ordinary reflexive experience yet avoid the regress, some contemporary philosophers contend that self-consciousness is an unconscious higher-order perception, others that it is an unconscious, higher-order thought.[35] The other chal-

---

34   J. F. Herbart, "Psychologie als Wissenschaft" in *Sämtliche Werke*, Band 5, ed. K. Kehrbach (Langensalza: Beyer, 1891), 242f, 255f.

35   Rocco Gennaro (ed.), *Higher-Order Theories of Consciousness: An Anthology* (Amsterdam: Benjamins, 2004); David Rosenthal, *Consciousness and Mind* (New York: Oxford University Press, 2004).

lenge mentioned above is similar but draws on the apparent difficulty of locating any intrinsic features of experience within experience itself. It is as though consciousness were a camera or a film projector, never able to film itself or to project its very projecting onto the screen. Consciousness seems, as Moore famously words it, "diaphanous," "transparent."[36]

But, in the first place, there are self-conscious experiences where these scenarios and dilemmas plainly have no grip. When we are in some moods, e.g., elation or angst, the mood need not be an attitude towards any particular object, nor does it by any means escape us. The intransitive use of 'feel' – as in 'How are you feeling today?' – makes this clear. Similarly, we speak of being "in" a mood, not "having" a mood. Instead of experiencing ourselves as something over and against them, moods often suffuse our existence and everything that belongs to our worlds (the grief that overcomes us in mourning, for example, hangs like a pall over everything in our path). Yet we experience contentment or the blues as our own, no less than we experience a signature as our own, as we enter it on a document before a notary.

In certain moods, to be sure, the fit with our surroundings can be so stable and organic that we do not experience any differentiation from them. In these cases, our organic identities seem to mesh so

---

36   For a critical review of positions, see Amy Kind, "What's so transparent about transparency?" *Philosophical Studies* 115/3 (2003): 225-244.

completely with their environments that we do not even experience the fit.[37] Yet moods of frustration or anger, longing or hope, exuberance or remorse tell a different story. Such moods are patently self-conscious, anything but 'transparent' (in the contemporary philosophical sense of the term), and they are singularly unsusceptible to the regress-engendering subject-object model.

In all the cases mentioned, it seems perfectly possible, in fact, quite normal for me to be aware of having an experience – and, indeed, as mine – without reflecting upon it as a distinct object. One might argue, moreover, that reflection, to whatever extent it is trenchant, supposes this immediate sort of self-awareness, even if it is typically tacit. When shooting a basketball, for example, I am aware that I am taking the shot without any reflection on the fact.[38]

---

37   Dewey builds his aesthetics on this experience; see John Dewey, *Art as Experience* (New York: Minton, Balch, and Co., 1934), 13-19. Note, however, how such moods of deep contemplation or rapture resemble the commonplace experience of someone walking in a way so perfectly adapted to senses of gravity and resistance that she takes no note of it (in contrast to the experience of walking in a pool).

38   So, too, localized experiences of the interoceptive variety (headaches) and those of the exteroceptive variety (blows to the midsection) are arguably immediate, self-conscious experiences prior to reflection. See Klaus Düsing's magisterial *Selbstbewußtseinsmodelle* (München:

In this connection, it bears recalling that every perception contains synchronically and diachronically tacit features that are no less present and, indeed, operative than what is explicit. These features contribute substantially to the time-space of a person's organic identity and the purposively recursive outreach characteristic of the personal experience of living. The purpose pursued, meanwhile, may be anything but explicit, particularly if I am pursuing a means to it. Though tacit, these features make up my experience and, hence, are necessarily part of any genuine self-awareness that I might have.

An example may help illustrate how these tacit features enter into our self-awareness. In a game of basketball, those features include such synchronically tacit features as the positioning and movement of the other players as well as that of my own body in the act of shooting (my explicit present). Diachronically tacit features of having the ball passed to me (the immediate, tacit past) and trying to score (the immediate, tacit future, namely, what I project, what I anticipate for the sake of the team and for my sake as a member of it) are no less in play. I am aware of myself – the very person taking the shot – not only throughout the process but also in terms of the

Fink, 1997); Uriah Kriegel, *Subjective Consciousness: A Self-Representational Theory* (Oxford: Oxford University Press, 2009); and Sean Gallagher and Daniel Zahavi, "Phenomenological Approaches to Self-Consciousness," *Stanford Encyclopedia of Philosophy* (online, 2014).

entire process. If I make the shot or I miss, I may be able to say immediately why, but only if asked (the pass came too slowly, I did not receive the pass in the right spot, I rushed the shot, I was fouled, etc.). If I am asked, I am sometimes able to identify a series of steps as mine without flinching, though without having previously paid attention to them, let alone made them explicit.[39]

As in this example, the content of experiences that I count as mine is, to be sure, often no different from that given to anyone else or at least to a certain group. (No one with healthy vision is excluded from experiencing a blue sky; the experience of minding a certain gap is given only to riders on the London Tube). But even when I share in these generic or specific experiences, there is something distinctive about the way their contents are given to me, something that renders them experiences for me – and no one else.[40]

This appeal to tacit features of experiences does not suppose a transcendent self, if the latter is supposed to transcend (lie outside) the timeliness of a life. But it does suppose what it reveals, namely, a

---

39   See the examples of "the correlation of self-feeling with purposeful activity" in Charles H. Cooley, *Human Nature and the Social Order* (New York: Schocken, 1902[1], rev. ed. 1964), 178.

40   Uriah Kriegel and Dan Zahavi, "For-Me-Ness: What It Is and What It Is Not" in *Philosophy of Mind and Phenomenology*, 36-53.

unity and homogeneity to the sort of experiences involved and my identification with them, i.e., the recognition that the experience and the recognition itself belong to me as one and the same and to no one else. This identity does not foreclose gaps in experiences, interruptions in the stream of consciousness. Yet there are sufficient similarities, repetitions, and patterns detectable in experiences for me to recognize myself both in my past and in my projects, both in what I have become and anticipate being and doing.

***

Shakespeare's exhortation to authenticity, the charge to be true to ourselves, presumably supposes the possibility of understanding ourselves truthfully. But there are natural and speculative challenges to doing so. Along with the possibility of being mistaken or ignorant about myself, the surfeit and transience of characteristics that may be identified with me, by myself or others, present challenges to self-understanding. The transience of those characteristics in particular gives rise to an influential speculative challenge to the very viability of personal identity, understood as an identity across time. The apparent transparency of consciousness presents a further speculative challenge, as does the supposed regress entailed by any form of self-consciousness.

The natural challenges of fallibility and ignorance, surfeit and transience contain the seeds of legitimate constraints on self-understanding. It is simply impossible for me to understand myself in terms of all the things that, under one description or another, it is legitimate to claim that I have been, am, or will be. Yet it is possible to meet these natural, formidable challenges by demonstrating how the saliency of certain sorts of personal characteristics and the experiences of them are based upon a person's life and organic identity. Demonstrating that saliency dovetails with mounting the proper response to the speculative challenges, since they suffer from a tendency to consider experiences detached from their grounding – and, indeed, frequently self-conscious grounding – in the organic stability of a person's living body. In these experiences, there is always someone living at one level for herself, reaching purposively and thus affectively across temporal intervals and distances. Grounded as they are in this dynamic, human experiences can only be adequately understood in terms of the life of the person having them across time and space.

The position that I have been arguing for here is an attempt to avoid the extremes of affirming a timeless disembodied self-identity and denying self-identity altogether in favor of disjointed experiences, at best papered over by a fictional or narrative identity. My argument appeals to the experience of self-identity, provided by self-conscious experiences and to the way those experiences supervene on self-conscious experiences of the organic identity of my body. Underwriting both appeals is the fundamental consideration that real identity – which is far from being the antithesis of difference – supposes the differences that demarcate change. A self-conscious experience is an experience of my identity in this sense – directly or indirectly supervening on my organic identity.

To sum up, a human being has a body but, at least in some respects, the way she has it is different from most of the ways that she may be said to have something. She may, of course, have a different hair color from time to time just as she has on different blouses. But 'having' takes on a quite different meaning when we say that she has a baby, an orgasm, or a heart attack. In these cases her experiences of herself are inseparable from her experiences of her body, so much so that it may be more accurate to say that she is her body. Yet even if it is true that she is in some sense her body, the use of 'is' here should not be construed as an 'is' of identity. Rather she may be said to be her body analogous to the way she is said to be alive, namely, as the ever-present ground of anything else she might be or have. So, too, she can experience, understand, and, yes, even be true to herself only on the basis of her corporeal existence, even though her personal identity, like her self-understanding, by no means completely coincides with her organic identity (the life of her body).

2. Practical challenges

Up till now I have been mounting a case for thinking that a person's organic identity, together with certain experiences that directly supervene on it, is a key constituent of her personal identity. Yet personal identity encompasses far more than the organic identity on which it is grounded. Who we are is also the product of a raft of interpersonal, historical experiences. The characteristics produced by these experiences are, like my brain, even more integrally a part of me than my big toe is. Nor is the reason for this importance a mystery. Participation in an historical matrix of interpersonal arrangements, collective structures, and social interactions is indispensable to human life and its embodied experience – not least to the practices by means of which a person sustains herself (finding nourishment, mating, and warding off threats) and, where possible, flourishes. Thanks to this matrix, our sexuality, our means of communicating and expressing ourselves, our ways of thinking, and our plans and opportunities are all at once personal and cultural. In this way and countless others, each of us comes to have a personal history, i.e., a "life-time," that rests not only on our individual biological lives but on the history (the life, if you will) of a community.

One salient reason that a person's identity is not reducible to the field of her self-understanding is, as noted earlier, the role others play in constituting her identity.[41] Her identity includes characteristics that she considers part of herself and those that others consider part of her – characteristics that obviously need not and, indeed, in some respects cannot be the same. Her consideration of herself, including the historical dimension of her past and her prospects, emerges from a position (the field of self-understanding) occupied by her alone. From that position she has access to only some of the characteristics that make her who she is, since who she is (again, including where she comes from and where she is likely headed) depends on others' views of her no less than on her own view of herself. Others often have access to characteristics that escape her – including characteristics that are as true of her (often in defining ways) as those to which she alone has access. Not surprisingly, she may balk at times at others' assessment or they may balk at hers. At this point, the difference in perspective becomes an opposition, and her identity is composed of opposing conceptions, each with its own *prima facie* integrity.

As long as that opposition falls along default lines of internal and external perspectives (her view of herself and others' view of her), her self-understanding and, with it, her sense of her personal identity

---

41   Recall that the field of self-understanding is exclusively composed of self-conscious experiences, whereas my identity includes both events of my organic identity below the threshold of experience and others' actual and potential views of me.

appears relatively straightforward. Yet there are obvious reasons to question this picture. Despite the integrity of our organic identities, we are not thrown into the world alone. Someone gave birth to us and, for the most part, we not only continue to exist but first come to awareness and, indeed, self-awareness through interaction with our mothers, fathers, families, and family friends. The field of a person's self-understanding (her internal perspective) is accordingly in large part a product of social factors specific to her upbringing and interactions with others. But then just how profoundly do these interactions define her individually? Does their reach leave any room for meaningful talk of her 'own' identity, for the injunction to be true to her self? Or is the injunction itself – like the idea of a self distinct from these interactions – yet another contrivance of society?

The social make-up of self-understanding gives us, in effect, reason to question the notion that the opposition between a person's view of herself and others' views of her amounts to a conflict between internal and external perspectives. A person often experiences these opposing perspectives in fact as a struggle within herself (with herself). Analogues with Hegelian dialectic and Nietzschean self-overcoming are patent. But if diverse perspectives vie with one another in the same field of a person's self-understanding, how does she sort them out or deal with them in a way that leaves any meaning to efforts to be true to herself?[42] And how does she know that the sorting is not itself simply the result of her place in society in this historical period? "To thine own self be true!" rings hollow if the self in question, far from being a person's own, is nothing more than a social construct, an epiphenomenon of history.

In the modern context, the rise of diverse social and historical explanations and critiques of human behavior, consciousness, and self-consciousness has contributed to a growing skepticism about the meaningfulness of Shakespeare's exhortation. Notably, on this score, economic theorists from across the political spectrum – both "vulgar Marxists" and their counterparts bent on applying behaviorist principles to advertising and marketing – often joined hands in their commitment to the possibilities of filling up the tabula rasa of individual human consciousness with socio-economic prerogatives. Quite apart from these earlier approaches, moreover, contemporary social psychologists have advanced the case for viewing the self as a social construction.[43]

---

42   By 'deal with them,' I have in mind a process of moving beyond them (by way of transforming them or simply leaving them behind), motivated by the opposition itself. Here, too, the challenge glossed here persists, since the entire process can be inherent to a socialization.

43   Kenneth J. Gergen, "The Self as Social Construction," *Psychological Studies* 56/1 (January-March 2011): 108-16. For a review of Gergen's views, along with those of

Yet one does not have to endorse the somewhat antiquated notions that the self is nothing more than a set of responses ("a reaction mass") to social stimuli[44] or that the notion of a self with properties of its own is modeled on a bourgeois commitment to the right of private property,[45] in order to appreciate that conscious and self-conscious experience has, seemingly down to its roots, a social make-up.[46] But there is also insufficient reason to plunge headway, as social constructionists typically do, into a murky ontology where, to put it mildly, relations somehow have a more fundamental status than the relata (with the implication that human individuals play second fiddle to society).

In contrast to the speculative challenges to self-understanding discussed in the first part of this study,

---

Geertz, Rorty, and Foucault, see Charles Guignon, *On Being Authentic* (New York: Routledge, 2004), 58-60.

44   John B. Watson, *Psychology from the Standpoint of a Behaviorist* (Philadelphia: Lippincott, 1919), 396ff, 420.

45   Theodor Adorno, *Zur Metakritik der Erkenntnistheorie* (Frankfurt am Main: Suhrkamp, 1970), 219-222; *Negative Dialektik* (Frankfurt am Main: Suhrkamp, 1966), 72, 188.

46   Goethe, *Tasso*, Akt 2, Scene 3: "Der Mensch erkennt sich nur im Menschen, nur das Leben lehret jedem was er sei." Cooley, *Human Nature and the Social Order*, 179: "The social self is simply any idea, or system of ideas, drawn from the communicative life, that the mind cherishes as its own."

the challenges now being considered are based, not upon the difference between our organic identities and our experiences of ourselves, but upon the slightness if not lack of any apparent difference between those experiences and their social make-up. In that sense they constitute practical challenges to the very idea of "one's own true self," though they are largely motivated by modern theories of the self as something socially constructed. In what follows I address these challenges in terms of what social theorists roundly consider the key to our social identities: institutional practices.[47]

*** * ***

---

47   Language is the pre-eminent institutional practice; indeed, for Mead it is foundational for individuals, their experiences, and their intelligence; George H. Mead, *Mind, Self, and Society*, (Chicago: University of Chicago Press, 1934), 47-69, 141n3, 223, 225, and Jürgen Habermas, *Theorie des kommunikativen Handelns*, Band II (Frankfurt am Main: Suhrkamp, 1981¹, 1995). Without mention of Mead, Searle also construes language as "the primary social institution...constitutive of institutional reality" and "the foundation of all other institutions," touting his account as alone explaining exactly how it is; John Searle, *Making the Social World* (Oxford: Oxford University Press, 2010), 109f. In order to keep this study within reasonable limits, I refrain from critical review of these approaches to language and from consideration of the role language broadly plays in forming social identity.

Our basic experiences of ourselves (and thus our prospects of self-understanding) experientially supervene, I argued above, on our organic identities. But these basic experiences are, as social theorists rightly see, highly plastic. Drinking to quench thirst and eating to satisfy hunger are basic ways of experiencing ourselves (the purposively recursive character of our experience) but there are a variety of ways to do this, largely determined by social institutions (from *Leviticus* 11: 2-7 to the FDA and EPA). In this manner society presupposes our organic identities by transforming and channeling their functions into institutional practices. In other words, just as our basic experiences supervene on our respective organic identities, so, too, the everyday and its social make-up supervene on those basic experiences.

It is no less true, as noted earlier, that our organic identities themselves suppose society. The ways that we live out our sexuality require interaction with others, as do the prospects of nourishing ourselves and surviving from infancy. Within the very broad constraints of preserving a human being's organic identity, there is, as history and anthropology amply confirm, a wide variety of ways that society may shape human experiences and how a human being experiences herself.[48]

---

48   As often noted, biology alone apparently cannot explain the difference between nomadic and agrarian lifestyles; Peter Berger & Thomas Luckmann, *The Social Construction of Reality* (New York: Anchor, 1967), 47.

The import of these considerations, however, is not simply the apparently trivial observation that there is no society without individual human beings and vice versa (although I think it is an observation not given its due). The import is rather a dynamic process of socialization involving the following (three) factors.[49] Thanks to their organic identity (not least their sexuality), human beings constantly reach out to one another. Over time, this process (their ways of coming together) comes to have an objective status of its own, not unlike and, indeed, not apart from the environments that they find themselves in. This objective status takes the form of institutions. Institutions are ways of doing things in a world that we share with others, thanks to surroundings ready-made for those purposes, largely through the efforts of previous generations of that society.[50] In economic insti-

---

49   The process involves externalization, objectivation, and internalization. In the ways that individuals externalize/express themselves, they produce societies; society assumes an objective status in the form of institutions that enlist and confront individuals, only to be internalized by them.

50   Mead, *Mind, Self, and Society*, 162: "A person is a personality because he belongs to a community, because he takes over the institutions of that community into his own conduct." The institutions are established over time by a society or culture as ways for its members to relate to the environment and to each other; Arnold Gehlen, *Der Mensch, seine Natur und seine Stellung in der Welt* (1940[1], Bonn: Athenäum, 1950[4]), 84; and *Urmensch*

tutions in particular, technology has always played a significant role, requiring individuals (e.g., farmers, shepherds, miners, blacksmiths, woodsmen) to learn to wield and manage its tools. In the past century or more, as several observers have noted, technology's increasingly formidable role on massive scales is such that today it is less a matter of us learning to use the tools of technology and more a matter of adapting ourselves to – finding a place where we are always replaceable within – the advanced technologies that drive contemporary institutions (such as communication, commerce, and combat over the web).[51]

As these remarks suggest, institutions have a peculiar, even ironic sort of existence that is often particularly conspicuous in our experience of contemporary, technologically-driven institutions. On the one hand, the social world has a certain substance and structure thanks to the practices mandated by institutions to members of that world. Our social identities are tied to these institutional practices as the things that we have to do (or take ourselves as having to do), including the procurement of the particular resources and tools (means of production) required to do them. We would not be the individuals we are

---

und Spätkultur (Bonn: Athanaeum, 1956), 9, 21, 47, 129, 233; Karl-Otto Apel, "Arnold Gehlens 'Philosophie der Institutionen,'" *Philosophische Rundschau* 10/1-2 (1962): 1-21.

51   Max Horkheimer and Theodor Adorno, *Dialektik der Aufklärung* (Amsterdam: Querido, 1947).

without institutions and institutional practices that define us.[52] Yet, while everyday reality in the form of these institutions has a controlling, objective presence, the institutions exist only as long as members of society engage in the institutional practices. As historical products of human making, institutions – and with them, the identities they provide – can be undone. So, too, social identities, while historically constituted, are not fully determined by institutions (a point to which I return below).

Yet institutions exist, at least in part, to lessen the burden of various requisite tasks by distributing them across society. They exist, in other words, to fulfill some social function, and that function is, by definition, a purpose shared by the individuals in that society, whether they are aware of it or not. (The internet, for example, has become an institution so vital to the contemporary social order that only someone bent on destroying that entire order

---

52 As an "agglomeration" of institutions, the everyday world has its own time-space, existing before and outside the individual whose own life is in certain respects an episode within the episode of its society. For someone born into the pre-Civil War South, for example, the institution of slavery is the everyday, already there in full force, with an inertia seemingly akin to natural events. The seemingly ineradicable vestiges of racism, long after that world's demise, suggest that transformations of social realities are typically matters of degree; on the maintenance and transformations of institutions, see Berger & Luckmann, *The Social Construction of Reality*, 147-63.

and ready to live without the benefits of the internet would have any interest in shutting it down en masse.) In this sense, institutions lend a kind of pragmatic order to everyday life, a life that we at once experience and constitute through institutional practices. (Thus, some form of the division of labor belongs among the most primitive and obvious instances of institutionalization.) In more or less stable situations where war or scarcity, for example, have not wreaked havoc with the institutions, the everyday practices engaged in by members of society ensure the fulfillment of those social functions. Institutions allow us to go about our business with one another; they provide us with the wherewithal to accomplish goals and negotiate the pursuit of them with others, whether intimately or at arm's length. In this sense, marriage is an institution as are, respectively, the stock market, the military, the internet, higher education, and so on.[53]

Not something given with a human being's organic identity or its environment, society's objective sta-

---

53 The range of institutions in which we participate everyday, i.e., those that we experience by reproducing them, is as vast and interconnected as it is pervasive. Not a day passes in which we are not playing some role in a complex of sexual, familial, educational, economic, technological, political, religious, recreational, and/or artistic institutions. Thanks to this engagement we find and define ourselves as wives and husbands, mothers and fathers, teachers, workers, car-drivers, voters, church-goers, boaters, musicians, and so on.

tus in the form of institutions has to be internalized via interactions, first with significant others ("primary socialization"), then with the "generalized other" ("secondary socialization").[54] The process of internalization is precisely the process in which the individual makes her own both the roles given to her and the attitudes exhibited by others. It is not, it bears stressing, as if the individual is fully formed before those interactions, i.e., before she learns that she is what she is called and how she is regarded (e.g., a girl, poor, disabled, brainy, a student, etc.). She may not understand herself, at least initially, in any other way. Something similar holds for every member of the society. Most of us have typical, more or less assigned places in the orderly world of social institutions. (Given the massive scale of the technological character of many institutions, internalization of them is today, as noted earlier, frequently a process of wholesale adaptation to their technologies.) We experience ourselves, for example, as consumers or

---

54   Berger & Luckmann, *The Social Construction of Reality*, 47-52, 60f, 129f, 180-83. To illustrate these two levels of socialization, Mead cites the difference between ordinary play (including playing at something, e.g., being a doctor) and a game where "the child must have the attitude of all the others involved in that game." Mead coins the term 'generalized other' to designate "the organized community or social group which gives to the individual his unity of self....The attitude of the generalized other is the attitude of the whole community" (Mead, *Mind, Self, and Society*, 135, 149-160, esp. 154).

producers, parents or spouses, spectators or performers, and so on. Living out these roles and the experiences they entail defines us – each of us individually.[55]

As noted above, the institutions themselves appear to successive generations (in contrast to their founders) as "the way things are done," as constant as the uniform changes in the seasons and no less a source of norms and normalcy.[56] For those born into these institutions, some account of their legitimacy and even sanctions are often necessary to maintain the institutional order they are supposed to provide.[57] Successful institutions manage to socialize individuals and exert authority over them in such a

---

55 As the reference to self-defining roles suggests, a person experiences the everyday world by performing these roles (engaging in the appropriate practices) of institutions of varying complexity, e.g., the roles of students, teachers, administrators in an academic institution. At the same time, thanks to her organic identity and her unique historical path, her personal identity encompasses and thereby exceeds her social identities. Personal identity and institutional selves, while never separate, remain distinct.

56 Berger & Luckmann, *The Social Construction of Reality*, 59; on the "objective reality" of institutions, confronting the individual as "undeniable facts," see ibid., 60.

57 Consider, for example, (a) biblical defenses of slavery, e.g., *Richmond Enquirer* (15 February 1820): "...whoever believes that the written word of God is *verity itself* must ... believe in the absolute rectitude of slave-holding," and (b) the penalties written into the *Fugitive Slave Acts* of 1793

manner that coercive measures give way, for the most part (though never completely), to internalization of the legitimating ideology. Conformity becomes habitual and spontaneous, as alternatives to the institutionalized ways of behaving appear increasingly meaningless or counterproductive.[58]

This sort of conformity makes for a kind of institutional inertia and, with it, a kind of social amnesia can set in, an obliviousness to the point of the practices. To be sure, for many institutional practices, there are special moments (e.g., initiating, celebratory, renewing) when the very fact that we perform them – as well as the reason why – takes center stage. For the most part, however, rote practice of even the most deliberate activity renders it a matter of habit, performed as mindlessly as the way we walk or chew our food. Mindless or not, engagement in

---

and 1850. On legitimation's importance, see Habermas, *Theorie des kommunikativen Handelns*, II, 188f, 270ff.

58   Accordingly, while never completely successful, one measure of the success of socialization and the everyday reality produced by it – i.e., symmetry between the objective and subjective realities (the internalization of objectified forms of social interaction) – is the degree to which it has become the norm throughout these upheavals and disruptions. See Berger & Luckmann, *The Social Construction of Reality*, 163-73; as Habermas aptly notes, however, Berger & Luckmann's Neo-Meadian model neglects the historical realities of economic and political struggles; Habermas, *Theorie des kommunikativen Handelns*, II, 170ff.

institutional practices provides a person with a social identity or, better, social identities. These identities are distinct from her organic identity, yet they inform her self-understanding and they are built into her personal identity. Again, who we are is based in part on these social identities, and for this reason we (our selves) are not identical to our bodies.

Yet a common thread runs through a person's organic identity, her experiences of herself directly supervening on that identity, and her social identity. Each exhibits a form of outreach that is, nonetheless, recursive by virtue of being purposeful (on the institutional level, think of flirting, betting, investing, teaching, working for a living). What distinguishes a person's social identity in this respect is the fact that a person's reflection back on herself passes through the eyes and ears of others. A person has a social identity "not directly, but only indirectly, from the particular standpoints of other individual members of the same social group."[59] These standpoints, as noted above, are more or less institutionalized in the form of roles and practices that define us.

---

59   Mead, *Mind, Self, and Society*, 138; ibid., 140: "The self, as that which can be an object to itself, is essentially a social structure, and it arises in social experience." Differentiating the self, so construed, from "subjective experience" and "consciousness," Mead emphasizes "the temporal and logical pre-existence of the social process to the self-conscious individual who arises in it" (ibid., 166-69, 186f).

The process of socialization glossed on the past few pages is by no means frictionless or flawless; nor is it by any means innocuous.[60] Competing interests and views of reality can violently clash; natural environments, resources, and means of production can prove recalcitrant or inadequate over time to the cultures and economies they once supported; irreconcilable differences between primary and secondary phases of socialization can occur along personal or familial, clannish or class lines; particularly given today's enormous, unprecedented technologies (think big data, genetic engineering, CO_2 emissions), reliance upon technological innovation can lead to unintended, tragic consequences. Institutions can liberate one segment of society at horrific cost to another. Moreover, the objective status of an institution may confront individuals as something external, even alien to them – even if it is their only means of not only maintaining, but asserting themselves.[61]

---

60   Theorists inevitably (often unknowingly) risk taking relatively stable states of their own societies or their idealization as baseline.

61   These institutions are both necessary and labile. Ideally, as noted above, they have a salutary, socially useful function but entire institutions or parts of them can fail miserably. Indeed, in a sense they can only succeed to a degree. As Simmel puts it, "an utterly fundamental dualism" is in play here. Yet while institutions tend to "a consolidation of their form," leading to "a more or less rigid prejudice" in their favor that renders them resistant to change, an analogous process takes place in each

Yet, for good or for ill, institutions are at the heart of the process of socialization. More importantly, for the purpose of these remarks, the way that institutional practices make up social identities refines the challenge that the process of socialization presents to Shakespeare's exhortation. It refines that challenge in at least two ways. First, how can the injunction to be true to herself make sense to someone if the only self she knows is the result of primary and secondary socialization? Does the injunction retain any meaning for a person if she (her identity) is defined or, better, if she defines herself by society's institutions and by the practices they set for her?[62] Secondly, if there are competing, ultimately incompatible social roles, how does she decide between them? How would she determine that carrying out one role is being true to herself or even just more true to herself than performing the other?[63]

---

individual; see Georg Simmel, *Soziologie. Untersuchungen über die Formen der Vergesellschaftung* (Leipzig: Duncker & Humblot, 1908), 587f.

62   That institutional norms may block the pursuit of authentic selfhood is one sort of concern; that there is no authentic self not reducible to a social matrix yet another. Consideration of a person's organic identity, her hand in forming her historical identity, and her unique good provide the means of addressing both concerns.

63   One might also ask whether an institutional identity disburdens a person in one respect only to alienate her in another. Habermas contends, notably, that we do not

***

Institutions are necessary; indeed, in many ways they are our only hope going forward. But they are also constantly a threat and not only to the prospects of being true to ourselves. Yet, before addressing that threat more specifically, we should not overlook the fact that there are oppressive institutions where the questions just raised may never surface or at least never be allowed to surface. I have in mind cases where institutional roles are thrust upon an individual, violently enforced, leaving an individual with no room to see herself in any other way or to define herself on something like her own terms. The institution of slavery is paradigmatic here, but something analogous occurs whenever a combination of institutions relentlessly keeps certain groups in such dire economic straits and/or oppressive social situations

---

have the distance from the form of life into which we have been socialized to make judgments about it. He approvingly cites Mead who remarks that, while a civilized human society provides a wider scope to non-conformity than primitive societies do, the individual's thinking and behavior "always and necessarily ... reflects ... the general organized pattern of experience and activity ... characterizing the social process in which he is involved." See Mead, *Mind, Self, and Society*, 221f and Habermas, *Theorie des kommunikativen Handelns*, 171. For a valuable critical review of Habermas' theory, see Hugh Baxter, *Habermas: The Discourse Theory of Law and Democracy* (Stanford, California: Stanford University Press, 2011), 9-59.

that they have little or no prospect of breaking out of them (consider, for example, widespread institutions of poverty, racism, exploitation, and discrimination).[64]

The existence of oppressive institutions underscores the fact that concern for being authentic is historically contingent upon institutions that allow the concern to arise. Relative to oppressive institutions (institutions of bondage), these institutions are more benign; that is to say, they are binding on individuals without recourse to bondage, albeit not without levels of coercion and the threat of coercion (legal, enforcement, and penal institutions). Indoctrination and education in primary and secondary stages of socialization, mentioned above, obviously play a dominant role in the maintenance of such institutions. Below I criticize a popular view that the concern for being authentic is, like these relatively more benign institutions, of modern vintage. But whatever the vintage, the concern can only arise in institutions and combinations of institutions that permit and even foster it, often benightedly. Thus, a clash of institutions is a typical catalyst for the concern. Antigone's fate, caught as she seems to have

---

64   Even under oppressive conditions, to be sure, rebellions occur (e.g., slave rebellions, peasants' revolts), even if they are the exception. Rebellion requires recognition that institutions are intolerable and replaceable, and a willingness – or sufficient desperation – to fight for the change.

been between the institution of the polis and the institution of the family, classically illustrates this dynamic; so does Lee's agony over upholding his sworn oath of allegiance to the United States or remaining faithful to his native state. Indeed, wherever a person finds herself embedded in staggered levels of institutions, each with a claim upon her and upon each other, the concern presents itself quite existentially.

If we set aside institutions whose recourse to bondage is their only means of maintaining themselves, the threat to being authentic can still arise from without and from within, i.e., from the practices and attitudes produced by the institutions themselves and from the very individuals that they are supposed to serve. The two sides of this threat correspond to two dialectically complementary ways in which personal identity (who a person is) presupposes institutions. It is one thing for a person to be identified with her institutional role, quite another for her to identify with it. Both identifications are in play in her personal identity, since an institution exists only if individuals carry out the practices and assume the roles specified by it and individuals exist only if institutions accommodate them. The crucial point here is that individuals and institutions or, better, the individuals within an institution exist in a symbiotic relation to one another. Each depends upon the other and, indeed, on the integrity of the other. An accurate self-understanding and an authentic existence are only possible within the parameters of this relationship. Yet this same symbiotic relationship provides occasions – again both from without and from within any individual – for thwarting this possibility.

The threat to authenticity from without presents itself when members of institutions in their attitudes and practices identify an individual solely with her role in an institution. In this way they overlook who she truly is (since she is not only someone fulfilling that institutional role) and, to that extent, they are incapable of respecting who she truly is. If those attitudes and practices become *de rigueur*, the institution is systematically repressive, conflating an individual's personal identity with a particular social identity that only makes up a part of it. The repression is perversely ironic, since the institution depends upon the actions of unique individuals who compose it. Those who are party to such an institution are, we might say, in bad faith, failing to acknowledge and even attempting to override individuals' responsibility for it, i.e., the fact that the institution only exists if an individual in each case does her job qua machinist, teacher, policeman, judge, etc. This repression of a person's uniqueness (not least her unique responsibility) can obviously take place to various degrees and on multiple levels. But to whatever degree it occurs, it sends a message that is rarely lost on the individuals involved. A person cannot help but internalize, at least to some degree, this sort of institutional disregard for her.

This last remark must be qualified, particularly if it leaves the impression that the threat to being authentic is mainly external. After all, when a person identifies with her institutional role (for good or for ill, depending upon the institution), she typically does so more or less self-consciously. It is by no means rare for the awareness to creep in, over time, that she has more than a little to do with producing that identity (becoming a spouse, a mother, a teacher, etc.). If, as I have been arguing above, (a) a substantial part of a person's identity is based upon her distinct organic identity, coupled with those of her experiences that directly supervene on the latter, and (b) her personal identity incorporates more than one social identity (in addition to her organic identity), then her identification with an institutional role is necessarily partial. But perhaps the most compelling reason why any such identification is only partial is to be found in a person's cognizance of the fact that she is, in no small degree, responsible for fashioning fundamental features of her identity.[65]

Far from being simply philosophical musings, the foregoing considerations correspond to concrete experiences, familiar to most of us, as we navigate our way from one set of institutionally determined interactions to another. My organic identity and my experiences of pain (the pain in my left leg) take

---

65 The *a priori* of social life is that "life is not entirely social"; individuals compose society by "standing inside it and outside it at once" (Simmel, op. Cit., 36-40).

center stage as I deliberately adopt the posture of a patient in my doctor's office; I put on my teacher's hat as one of my students enters my office; I kiss my wife's cheek when I come home; I do a father's duty as I ask my son if he's finished his homework. It is commonplace, in other words, for us to identify ourselves individually with institutional roles and take responsibility for doing so. We practice what institutions dictate, all the while aware (a) that our individual identities are not confined to any particular social role, any cohort of such roles, or even the ensemble of all such roles, and (b) that these institutional practices and corresponding identities at every step require our compliance.

This point can be put in more general, abstract terms: A person cannot identify herself with a role without being different from it, without having an identity apart from the role. Her awareness of that identity, i.e., her difference from the role, is not, it bears repeating, an idle awareness. It is an awareness of the difference that she makes, an awareness of the acts (practices) that she performs as part of her personal identity, without which neither the institution in question nor her corresponding social identity exist. It is the *practical* awareness, in other words, that she is co-responsible for the entire process.[66]

---

66   She need not have this awareness, of course, though her personal identity remains distinct from her social identities. Personal identity encompasses (but is not limited to) a person's organic identity, social identities, and

To the extent that something like the foregoing analysis holds, individuals are not naively co-opted by institutions. They do not enter into interactions with others innocently, without a sense of their doing so and, thus, of their responsibility for doing so. The threat that the symbiotic relationship between institutions and individuals presents to being authentic is not merely external. Indeed, an individual is in bad faith, that is to say, she is responsible for refusing to acknowledge or, better, to exist as who she is when she accepts without resistance a repressive institution's pigeon-holing of her.[67]

---

corresponding experiences. It is not the empty suit of some liberal accounts of human subjectivity, removed from all social and historical traditions. The cases of Antigone and Lee illustrate how identifications with competing social roles can undo an individual. Nonetheless, insofar as a person learns to differentiate herself from them, institutions become a vehicle for a person's recognition of her freedom and responsibility. For discussion of this Hegelian insight, see Arnold Gehlen, "Über die Geburt der Freiheit aus der Entfremdung," *Archiv für Rechts- und Sozialphilosophie* XL/3 (1953): 351f.

67   Worry that identity is only a function of a social matrix is misbegotten if based upon an exclusive disjunction of a person's organic identity and her social identities. As noted above, a person's organic identity includes uniquely living out her sexuality with others and establishing social identities in the process. Creating her own historical identity in many other ways as well, she is true or not to potentialities that are authentically hers, while entailing

Earlier I suggested that this particular threat to being authentic comes from without and from within. The conjunction here is vague but deliberately so, given the symbiotic relationship of individuals and institutions mentioned earlier. Institutions, as inherited ways of interacting with one another, are necessary conditions for the development of an individual's social identities and, thereby, her personal identity. Since we cannot be authentic without having some access to our personal identity, institutions and being authentic go hand-in-hand.[68] But along with oppressive institutions (institutions of bondage), there are also repressive institutions. A repressive institution systematically attempts to override the uniqueness in decision and action on the part of individuals that is central to their identities, their self-understanding, and their prospects for existing authentically. Individuals can obviously play along, refusing to accept who they are by denying their uniqueness, including their unique complicity in the institutional process of socialization, whether by

---

sustained engagement in institutional practices (language, culture, family, etc.). Pre-eminent among those potentialities is that of rationally perceiving the good and, in the process, taking responsibility for that engagement.

68   Thus, a person's use of the first person to designate experiences of herself in social roles – e.g., the 'I do' in the wedding ceremony, 'I voted' in the general election, etc. – indicates that on some level they are not shared with anyone else.

blindly conforming, feigning the posture of dropping out, or adopting the pretense of ironically playing with the process (and these alternatives, of course, by no means exhaust the possible modes of self-denial).[69]

In this sense the individual, repressing her own individual identity and responsibility, can abet a society replete with repressive institutions. The result is a kind of social or institutional inertia that is inimical to being authentic, propped up not only by strata in society with an interest in maintaining repressive institutions and the power to do so, but also by individuals' languor and comfortableness of not accepting responsibility for them.[70] As for the latter, Sartre's portrayal of a waiter in bad faith comes to mind; he is inauthentic because he is, he knows, responsible for letting himself be defined as a waiter and nothing more. But we can also imagine someone whose only opportunity for employment is work of sheer drudgery becoming utterly disillusioned with her lot. Or someone so disadvantaged physically or by her surroundings and upbringing that her over-

---

69   The flurry of discussions unleashed by Christy Wampole's account of hipsters provides a case study of one such response; see "How to Live Without Irony" in *Opinionator: A Gathering of Opinion from Around the Web, New York Times* (November 17, 2012).

70   Social theory, too, can contribute to these standing threats by overstating the roles of the institutions or the individuals.

whelming motivation is to escape from who she is. I mention these extreme but hardly rare cases merely to underscore that the challenge to being authentic arising from the process of socialization contains elements that are typically both internal and external, both serendipitous and deliberate.

We can begin to appreciate what it means to be authentic by considering what is necessary to respond to these challenges. The project of being authentic requires attainment of a level of maturity with respect to a person's social identities, beginning with the recognition that they are only a part of her personal identity.[71] But it also entails the recognition of both those social identities and the degree of complicity on her part relative to them. A person's level of maturity in this regard corresponds to the degree to which she not only owns up to her role in the institutions, but also takes seriously her responsibility relative to them (she may re-commit herself to the institution in question or abandon it).

So far, my account of having a mature social identity encompasses three characteristics: being different from, but accountable for, the institutions determining that identity (without necessarily the pretension of a view from nowhere institutionally); a cognizance of that difference and accountability (or, alternatively, one's unique accountability); and a

---

71   Alternatively, it requires showing that 'authenticity' is not merely code for a transition from sort of one institutional identity to another.

demonstrated willingness to act on that cognizance, i.e., to take responsibility for one's accountability for the institutions (whether by deliberately re-affirming or dismantling them, revising or abandoning institutional practices). Developing a mature social identity plays a fundamental role in being authentic inasmuch as it requires accepting and acting on the truth about a person's social identity, including her difference from that identity and her responsibility for the latter.

Underdetermined to a fault in this gloss, however, are the implications of taking responsibility for social identity. In order to take responsibility, it is necessary to question the purpose of the institutions themselves and their practices. Recall that, formally considered, institutions are ways for individuals to interact with each other and these ways of interacting are instituted for some purpose. For a person to become mature in her social identity, she has to consider both what purpose an institution is supposed to fill (the reason why it or something like it is or should be instituted), and whether it continues to fulfill that purpose. In other words, a person cannot take responsibility for her social identity without determining ideal or at least desirable but realizable forms of interaction with others. Moreover, those determinations, like her personal identity, must not be confined to interactions peculiar to a particular society or culture.

***

At this point the response to the practical challenge to authenticity, as it arises from the process of socialization, may seem to have hit the skids in two respects. First, how can we hope to determine the appropriate forms of interaction in a way that is not rooted in the culturally specific processes of internalization that form our social identities? Second, how can recourse to an ideal have anything to do with being true to ourselves? Talk of an ideal, even a realizable ideal, seems pointedly at odds with a concern for authenticity. What I've been calling 'Shakespeare's exhortation' is, after all, Polonius' counsel to his son, presumably beckoning him to be true to where he comes from. In other words, when Polonius urges his son: "to thine own self be true," he more likely means something like "be true to your roots, uphold your family name" or at least "trust your own instincts and intuitions." At any rate, Polonius is not exhorting him, it would seem, to be true to an ideal, to what he ought to be.

The key to the answer to the first of these questions (which echoes questions at the outset of this second segment) is human beings' distinctive capacity for reason. A person's exercise of this capacity in discerning who she is, socially and otherwise, is the mark of someone with a mature personal identity, precisely because this exercise is essential to who we authentically are (and can become). As mentioned earlier, rationality is in general an interpretive capacity that emerges, along with imagining and thinking, at the intersection of memories and anticipations, motivated and guided by desires. Thanks to the affectivity of desires – whether in the form of hunger, thirst, lust or fear – a person reaches out for food or partners, to fight or take flight. Recalling means of satisfying such desires and anticipating similar satisfaction, I perceive one thing as edible, then another, and then perhaps a third thing that is inedible. The first two may be the same sorts of things, e.g., two apples, or different sorts of things, e.g., an apple and a grape. Either way, I entertain something common, something that specifies what is perceived but is not confined to it. I have images of apples and the thought of being an apple which is not the same as the image. Something similar applies to thoughts of what is edible.

Reasoning supposes a capacity to entertain such common features afforded by perception (to think in general terms or universals, if you will) and relate them to one another. From experiences of the common features of apples in the past, I recognize (perceive) apples in the present and anticipate (infer) experiencing those same sorts of features again. A further rational step would involve consideration of what is common to apples and grapes, a concept of edibility. But, along with its capacity to recognize and entertain what is common (i.e., both the common feature and its instances), reason is also able to recognize and entertain what is not (e.g., certain mushrooms are not edible). Inference in general supposes recognizable commonalities and differences. (If it's an apple or grape, go ahead and eat it; if it's a Jack O'Lantern mushroom, don't.)[72]

This capacity to recognize and anticipate is the work of reason *in nuce* – and it is work, practically directed at some end (e.g., satisfying hunger without poisoning ourselves). Just as there is a hierarchy to such practices (I may need to climb the tree to get to the apple), so reason can engage in higher or lower levels of this sort of instrumental reasoning. But it can also consider the complex of things and their common features as a whole, apart from any specific problem-solving or particular human purpose. In Aristotle's classic account, this contemplative kind of rationality typically requires the ability to withdraw from practical activities and consider things at leisure.

Although truncated to a fault, this gloss hopefully puts a spotlight on how the power of reasoning enables human beings to think in ways not confined to their particular situations, whether based upon their organic or social identities. They are able to consider various types of things, events, practices, relationships, and dispositions that are found across cultures and epochs. So, too, they are able to consider them-

---

72   Although my gloss stresses practical reasoning and inferences, theoretical reasoning supposes similar structures. Stripped to the basics, formal laws of inference also come down to generalization and negation.

selves both as individuals and human beings, and not simply as members of this or that institution or society. They are able to examine institutions and societies critically, to evaluate human beings' prospects of surviving and flourishing in them, to consider what makes a certain sort of interaction purposeful, and what makes a particular institution reasonable across cultures, societies, and epochs.[73]

Just as biology studies the organic character of human beings in a way not confined to any particular culture and, in contrast to biological engineering, without concern for any instrumental use of the knowledge gained, so human rationality provides the wherewithal to investigate what is invariant to successful (purposeful, rational) types of interactions and, indeed, to do so non-instrumentally. A person is mature in her social identity, i.e., she possesses the sort of identity that is consistent with being authentic, when she evaluates institutions accordingly and acts on those rational evaluations.[74] To be sure, ratio-

---

73   To be sure, much of experience is tied to the more or less mindless exercise of socially inculcated habits, but without precluding someone from developing these or other habits because she realizes, through the use of reason, that it is good (purposeful) to do so.

74   Echoing Kant, Adorno also stresses the notion of maturity in connection with human rationality; see his *Erziehung zur Mündigkeit - Vorträge und Gespräche mit Hellmut Becker 1959 bis 1969*, ed. Gerd Kadelbach (Frankfurt am Main: Suhrkamp, 1971), 109: "Mündigkeit

nal evaluations along these lines admit of many levels of sophistication, relative to a person's individuality and experience, her habits of reflecting suitably on those experiences, and her theoretical competencies. (Historians, anthropologists, economists, and neurologists are each able to bring a different sort of theoretical competency to bear on understanding human nature. So, too, given an individual's personal experiences, she will understand human nature from a unique perspective.) But the beginning of such evaluations in any case is a matter of getting clear about the human purposes that the institutions are supposed, by past or present society, to fulfill. The evaluation is only complete when a person comes to a reasoned conclusion that fulfilling those purposes does or does not advance human existence, prospects for human beings, individually and collectively, to survive and flourish.[75]

---

bedeutet in gewisser Weise soviel wie Bewußtmachung, Rationalität. Rationalität ist aber immer wesentlich auch Realitätsüberprüfung, und diese involviert regelmäßig ein Moment der Anpassung. Erziehung wäre ohnmächtig und ideologisch, wenn sie das Anpassungsziel ignorierte und die Menschen nicht darauf vorbereitete, in der Welt sich zurechtzufinden. Sie ist aber genauso fragwürdig, wenn sie dabei stehenbleibt und nichts anderes als ,well adjusted people' produziert, wodurch sich der bestehende Zustand, und zwar gerade in seinem Schlechten, erst recht durchsetzt."

75　There are enormously complicated issues besetting such inferences, from questions of the meanings of

One might suppose, for example, that an economic institution exists to insure a production and distribution of goods in sufficient quantity to satisfy the basic needs of the members of the society. If hunger is prevalent in that institution, if poverty itself is institutionalized within it, or if it survives only through oppressing or repressing someone somewhere, then the institution is plainly a failure. And, of course, a person would be inauthentic were she to recognize that the institution in this crucial sense miscarries but fail to say or do anything herself to change it. In a similar way, she would be inauthentic were she to recognize and yet do nothing to combat institutional inequities and violations of standards of fairness that are hardly matters of convention alone.[76]

This last reference to Aristotle's claim that a part of justice is natural (not conventional) should give us pause, however, given the long tradition of finding this claim reconcilable with putatively natural justifications of institutions of enslavement and prejudice. The tendency to identify or, better, confuse the natural with the cultural can be overwhelming, partic-

---

'survival' and 'flourishing' to questions of the meaning of 'collective' humanity (e.g., intergenerational justice).

76   Aristotle, *Nicomachean Ethics*, Book V (1134b18-35). As these remarks make clear, acting ethically goes hand-in-hand with being true to our social selves. Being authentic is equivalent, in other words, to projecting inherently shared possibilities that make up a common good, instrumentally or intrinsically.

ularly given the rhetorical advantages, not least the empowering authority, of allegedly speaking from a higher standpoint. Careful consideration of the interactions in the past and in widely different cultures may not be sufficient to keep this tendency in check. Any success we might have in evaluating institutions on the basis of human nature cannot forego subjecting the criteria of those evaluations to the study of history and other cultures. Nor can consideration of these criteria ignore the naturalness of technology and other forms of human innovation, production, and construction.

Nonetheless, at least the outline of an answer to the first question raised above (about our capacity to break out of the parochial bounds of our own social identities) is to be found in rationality as a specific, natural capacity of human beings. As the capacity to recognize essential patterns among different ways of living and to make inferences accordingly, reason also provides us with the means to a mature social identity. The answer to the second question raised above (the putative conflict between being true to who we are and some conception of who we ought to be) can be found, again in outline-form at least, in the character of this and other human capacities. In the account given above, rationality is a capacity exercised in the process of interpretation that takes place at the intersection of memories and anticipations, guided by desire.[77] This process, involving imagination and thought, typically exhibits the same sort of purposively recursive outreach typical of a person's organic identity as well as the experiences that directly supervene on it. Who we are is not independent of processes of constantly and recursively reaching out to our surroundings in ways that, in combination, are purposeful, i.e., good, for the organism. To isolate the process or an experience of the process from this general dynamic is to misrepresent what it is or, in our case, who we are. In other words, *who-we-are* is not separate from distinct possibilities that make up our distinctive purposes, i.e., *what is good for us*. What is good for us, moreover, determines what we ought to do and be. Being true to who-we-are is accordingly inseparable from doing what we ought to do and being who we ought to be. To be true to ourselves is, in short, to be who we ought to be.

Our personal identities, like our organic and social identities, are unfinished, but they are unfinished because they've begun – and begun, moreover, not as some mass of indeterminate possibilities but as a complex of determinate potentialities. Part of the determinateness of those potentialities consists in the fact that their realization is purposive, i.e., good

---

77   This claim does not rule out a purely theoretical pursuit of knowledge. Such a pursuit must itself be desired (indeed, such that desire of this pursuit must motivate a shaping of other sorts of desires).

for us, and realizable through the right use of reason. As long as we exist, part of our identity consists in having, projecting, and realizing those potentialities, pursuing those purposes (goods), to various degrees in rationally appropriate ways.[78] Hence, to be true to ourselves is precisely to be in pursuit of those goods, the achievement of which would be, of course, ideal.[79]

These considerations forestall an otherwise trenchant criticism of Shakespeare's exhortation, the criticism, namely, that it does not preclude someone from being wholeheartedly sinister or villainous. There obviously are psychopaths and sociopaths, individuals with, as the medical profession puts it, an

---

78 This point is a truism in the case of our organic identities, each of which consists in a continual process of actualizing specific potentialities for sustenance, growth, repair, reproduction, and flourishing at levels mostly below the threshold of consciousness (in the face, to be sure, of an impending decline). But the point is no less a truism in the case of our social identities and, I suggest, our personal identities as well. We exist and have our identities, socially and individually, by constantly projecting possibilities for ourselves, determined in part by our traditions. We do so, not indiscriminately, but purposively, with a view to some good.

79 Just as Hume was wrong to think that experiences are fundamentally disjointed, requiring imagination to associate them with one another, so he was wrong to think that we do not experience determinate potentialities that enable us, within certain parameters, to derive what ought to happen from what is.

"antisocial personality disorder" who may convince themselves that they are being true to themselves by inflicting pain of one sort or another on others.[80] Yet we have ample reason to think that, as long as a person is in such a state of mind, she is not true to herself, to who she fundamentally is, since being human and acting humanely is essential to who she most basically is. In other words, she is not guided by rational desires (and rationality is by no means limited by our organic identities or to their distinctive spheres).

3. The existential challenge

In my previous remarks I have addressed two sorts of challenges to Shakespeare's exhortation. The challenges making up the first set were largely *speculative*, drawing a bead on the very plausibility of personal identity, based upon aspects of the *nature* of conscious experiences (their intermittence) and consciousness (its transparency). The challenges making up the second set were, by contrast, of a more *prac-*

---

80   See "Antisocial Personality Disorder: Official Criteria" in American Psychiatric Association, *Diagnostic and Statistical Manual on Mental Disorders*, fifth edition (2013), 301.7 (F60.2). To suggest that the psychopath acts rationally, given her desires, is to misconstrue rationality as purely instrumental and to fail to recognize the difference between desires in line with her authentic potential and desires that are not. Avoiding these misconstruals entails care for the psychopath, not condemnation.

tical nature, contesting the possibility of being authentic given how extensively *social* practices shape a person's identity. I have tried to present reasons to question both sorts of challenges, either because they misconstrue the underlying corporeal character of our experiences – not least those that are intrinsic to preserving or furthering our lives (and the organic identity of our respective bodies) – or because they neglect the ways in which our social identities depend upon aspects of ourselves – not least our powers of reasoning – that cannot be reduced to those identities. Underlying the reasons presented is the basic contention that an individual's personal identity, while necessarily composed of her organic and social identities as well as her experiences, is more than the sum of them – not least because it entails an unfinished potentiality that supersedes them.

In presenting these reasons, I have relied heavily on a feature common to those identities, to the experiences she has of herself that directly supervene on her organic identity as well as her experiences of herself in particular social roles. That feature is what I have dubbed, somewhat clumsily, the 'purposively recursive outreach' of the processes and experiences peculiar to those identities. Whether reaching out to things to satisfy our basic, animal needs or reaching out to our co-workers to accomplish something, we experience ourselves both as the purposes of these actions and in the feedback from pursuit of them. At the organic level, the feedback mechanisms are automatic, but the attempts to quench my thirst or to signal a fellow driver that I intend to turn are no less so. Multiple processes below the threshold of experience proceed without interruption (as long as we are alive) while experiences of them are intermittent. This fact suffices to establish the difference between a person's organic identity and her experiences of herself. Yet they share a common purposively recursive structure, and we have every reason to think that the latter supervene on the former. While a person's experiences of herself obviously do not coincide with her organic identity, they not only suppose it but structurally emulate it; in a sense, they express it. At the same time, insofar as social identities are tied to the survival, success, and morality of institutions (purposive forms of outreach themselves), they presuppose an engagement in institutional practices that is both unique and rational, i.e., not the result of those social identities alone.

Much more would need to be said, to be sure, to respond adequately to the challenges to authenticity addressed above. My aim has been merely to sketch a promising line of argumentation to contest them, based upon an alternative conception of personal identity that gives meaning to the pursuit of authenticity. Yet although the challenges that have been addressed are considerable (as can be gathered from contemporaries' continuing receptiveness to them), they do not present the biggest obstacle to following Shakespeare's injunction.

The primary challenge to authenticity is existential, arising from a deep-seated tendency to base our self-conceptions solely on a desire to have others view us positively. The challenge is personal. We can decide to yield to this tendency or to resist it, and we know, in our heart of hearts, that on some level we cannot escape making this decision. The challenge has the power to sabotage the attempt to be authentic because it bases our self-conception on a presumed relation to others – where the presumption trumps reality (the truth about ourselves). Despite some modern views to the contrary (disputed below), there is a long history of recognizing this threat. In Judeo-Christian terms, the threat takes the form of a temptation. But it is not just any temptation; it is, as Augustine puts it, "the most dangerous temptation, [stemming] from the love of praise," a temptation to which we have always already fallen prey more or less.[81]

Augustine provides a striking account of the perversity of this temptation, rooted as it is in a desire to be feared or loved by others, a desire that becomes inordinate when it strives to secure a joy that is, in reality, sheer phantasy.[82] A person thinks herself

---

81   Augustine, *Confessiones* X, 38.

82   Augustine, *Confessiones* X, 36: "...tertium temptationis genus...timeri et amari velle ab hominibus non propter aliud, sed ut inde sit gaudium, quod non est gaudium[.]" For Augustine, pride is perverse, in part because it is so elusive, leading him to comment that it leaves him

more or less estimable than she is in order to seem deserving of the esteem from others that she craves, the sort of esteem that warrants their fear of her or their affection for her. By giving in to that craving and crafting an image of herself to satisfy it, she is true, not to herself, but to what she thinks will win others' praise. Pride, so conceived, presents the supreme threat to being authentic.

***

---

uncertain (*incertum*), with almost no (*paene nulla*) capacity of examining it. Pride is elusive because of the pervasive role played by praise from others. After all, it is necessary for anyone occupying certain positions (*officia*) in human society – e.g., someone in the position of a bishop – to be loved and feared. Moreover, it would be not only abnormal, but simply wrong to do things that would make us detestable, so much is praise – and rightly so – "the companion of a good life and good works" (*bonae vitae bonorumque operum comes*). But if, then, I experience the praise that comes from living a good life, I do not experience its absence and, thus, cannot know whether I am oblivious to it. So, too, though he takes more delight in truth than in praise, it is obvious, Augustine adds, that others'"approval" (*suffragatio*) augments the joy he takes in any good he possesses and that he is less upset when others are unjustly praised than when he is (*Confessiones* X, 36-37). But the temptation's perverseness shows up, too, when someone praises herself for the good things bestowed on her as though she deserved it (ibid., 39) or prides herself for not being proud (ibid., 38).

Contemporary thinkers have recognized a version of this challenge to authenticity, albeit under supposedly competing and novel rubrics of sincerity and authenticity. According to Lionel Trilling, sincerity ("the avoidance of being false to any man through being true to one's own self") is a new element in the history of the moral life of Europe, as is this specific coinage of the term, supposedly not in use before Shakespeare. The same, he suggests, applies to authenticity, an idea that in turn allegedly displaces sincerity from its privileged status. These claims are remarkably parochial, brushing aside, as they do, a bevy of relevant ancient and medieval meditations on the virtue of being true to oneself.[83] Trilling mentions Aristotle's account of μεγαλοψυχία, for example, only in passing and completely ignores medieval treatments of the corresponding virtues.

---

83   Lionel Trilling, *Sincerity and Authenticity* (Cambridge, Massachusetts: Harvard University Press, 1972), 5, 13, 25. On Trilling's view, the 'self' in pre-modern writings – Aeschylus' γνῶθι σαυτόν, Hugh of St. Victor's "sapientia illuminat hominem ut seipsum agnoscat" (*Didascalicon de studio legendi*, I, 1) or even Abelard's *Ethica or Scito Te Ipsum*, to mention only a few examples – is allegedly used only reflexively and not as "an autonomous noun" referring to what someone "really and intrinsically" is. For development of Trilling's broadly Hegelian location of authenticity in the *Neuzeit*, see Bernard Williams, *Truth and Truthfulness: An Essay in Genealogy* (Princeton: Princeton University Press, 2002); and Guignon, *On Being Authentic*, Chapters 2-5.

Yet these complaints, while warranted, should not keep us from appreciating Trilling's insight into a prominent path taken by literature in modernity. He notes how a new antagonism to the heroic style (a staple of tragedy) arose in the Renaissance.[84] The heroic was regarded not only as absurd (unrealistic) but also a hindrance to the practical conduct of life. The trend – epitomized in the work of Cervantes, Fielding, and Swift – supposedly reflected an increasing concern with ordinary life and practices. But it also provided "the ground of a new, or rediscovered, kind of spiritual experience," giving rise to a new definition of the hero or, at least, to an emphasis on "an individual's experience of his existence…the sentiment of being."[85]

According to Trilling, Rousseau's belief in the individually and socially redeeming features of sincerity, exemplified in the project of his *Confessions*, is central to this development. Rousseau is said to display the sort of intense conviction of his sincerity and the truth of his own experience that allegedly grounds a newly awakened power and authority to criticize the political and social order. Yet Rousseau's project comes to grief, not simply because of its in-

---

84   Trilling, 87ff.

85   Don Quixote, Tom Jones, and Leopold Bloom exemplify the new sort of hero, while Rousseau's *le sentiment de l'être* is repeated in English by Wordsworth and echoed in Whitman's "the hardest basic fact and the entrance to all facts" (Trilling, 92).

sincerity (as many critics point out), but because Rousseau bases sincerity on a conception of an unadulterated, private, unified self. Naturally pure, this inner self is essentially bifurcated from society, corrupted by it, but also capable of reforming society by elaborating, teaching, and enforcing the duties of "honest individuals."[86]

According to Trilling and Bernard Williams, the figure of Rameau's nephew (in Diderot's work by that name) spectacularly supplies what Rousseau's conception of sincerity lacks, namely, a conception of a self, alienated down to its roots, and fully aware of the fact. The nephew is a parasitic but intelligent buffoon, alternately ingratiating and offending the segments of society from which he lives (barely). Yet all the while Rameau's nephew is not only "to an unusual degree sincere" but also seemingly authentic.[87] In the dialogue, he demonstrates that he is no different from "honest individuals," thereby exposing their insincerity and, with it, "the loss of personal integrity and dignity that the impersonations of social existence entail."[88]

---

86   Trilling, 23, 58f, 65ff, 74f, 92; Williams, 173-84.

87   Williams, 189; I write 'seemingly' since his authenticity lacks the steadiness, as Williams puts it, that marks the genuine authenticity (a steadiness characteristic, one might argue, of the virtue of magnanimity and humility, discussed below).

88   Trilling, 31.

Trilling claims that Diderot's portrait of the nephew is also meant "to suggest that moral judgment is not ultimate."[89] The claim seems rash and even untoward, given his view that Diderot draws the portrait to pass moral judgment on society. Yet the main point of the comparison between Rousseau and Diderot is to underscore a growing sense that sincerity is not enough, at least if it means – paraphrasing Williams' paraphrase of Hegel – feeling unreflectively at home in one's social environment. In addition to demonstrating that sincerity does not guarantee the purposes of virtue (as Rousseau seems to have thought) and that authenticity fares no better in this regard, Diderot's portrait of Rameau's nephew raises, in Williams' terms, "a more radical question, how far the self can be expected to be receptive to morality at all."[90]

Trilling draws the contrast between Rousseau and Diderot to illustrate how sincerity, supposedly the moral ideal of early modernity, gives rise in the 18th century to a different moral ideal, authenticity. While both he and Williams are short on specifics,

---

89   Trilling, 32. Trilling contends that Hegel stresses this intention in the course of incorporating the figure of Rameau's nephew into his account of "*der sich entfremdete Geist*," with the implication that "sincerity is undeserving of our respect"; Trilling, 46f; G. W. F. Hegel, *Die Phänomenologie des Geistes* (Hamburg: Meiner, 1988), 325, 345f, 360.

90   Williams, 190.

the difference between the two ideals seems to turn on the possibility that a person can deliberately convey to others what she takes her beliefs or feelings to be, while being mistaken, having false beliefs, or even having feelings irreconcilable with who, at some deeper level, she is. In this sense, she can be sincere, but inauthentic.

Trilling also casts the distinction in terms of the necessary role of expression in sincerity. Sincerity supposes an expression, and expression is distinct from the mindset responsible for the expression, allowing for a question of veracity to arise. In cases of authenticity, by contrast, the distinction cannot be meaningfully sustained. As a means of illustrating this difference, Trilling appeals to Wordsworth's depiction of Michael, the shepherd, who, having lost his son to the city, sits silently in the hills with his flock, expression-less. "There is no within and without: he and his grief are one."[91] 'Sincerity,' Trilling insists, simply does not suffice to capture this reality; 'authenticity' does.

> A very considerable originative power had once been claimed for sincerity, but nothing to match the marvelous generative force that our modern judgment assigns to authenticity, which implies the downward movement through all the cultural superstructures to some place where all movement ends, and begins.[92]

---

91   Trilling, 93.

92   Trilling, 12.

As this text makes clear, the fact that sincerity is bound to expression makes it, on Trilling's account, irretrievably beholden to cultural convention – the very conventions that make it possible for the sincere person to express feelings and beliefs to others. By contrast, authenticity is said to reach "as far down beneath the constructs of civilization as it was possible to go, the irreducible truth of man, the innermost core of his nature, his heart of darkness."[93] After registering how the acquisitive principle (having rather than being) and the mechanical principle were felt to be the enemy of this truth and "the source of inauthenticity," Trilling notes the shift in the early 20th century towards an embrace of "the beauty and vitality of the machine" – again, in the name of authenticity – and, with that embrace, a tendency to ascribe "absoluteness not to the universe but to the creative faculty of the artist."[94]

***

---

93   Trilling, 108; for glosses on Jung's and Freud's insight into this darkness, see Guignon 49-54.

94   Trilling cites Marx, Arnold, and Wilde as opponents of the acquisitive principle (Trilling, 122-25), Emerson, Carlyle, and Ruskin as opponents of the machine principle (Trilling, 126-27), and Martinetti as the herald of the machine (Trilling, 128-30) – in the name of authenticity in each case.

The accuracy of this version of the literary and political history of modern Western European ideas of
sincerity and authenticity is a matter of debate.[95] But
the historical narrative makes an important point,
namely, that these ideas have been seen to come
apart, that we can judge someone to be sincere yet
inauthentic (we can see, for example, even if she can't,
that she's acting this way – saying the right things,
candidly conveying her feelings – but only because
others expect it of her). Authenticity trumps sincerity, on this view, because the latter, in contrast to the
former, is inevitably co-opted by the social trappings
of its expression. It would seem, on this view, that
Shakespeare's exhortation to be true to ourselves
cannot, without further qualification, be an exhortation to sincerity.

Yet there are, I want to argue, several things wrong
with this conclusion. It overlooks the numerous ways
in which I can be true to myself only by being true
to others and vice versa. (If a friendship is essential
to who we authentically are or can be, then so, too,
is sincerity, since there can be no friendship without sincerity between friends.) Inauthentic sincerity
is all too common, to be sure, but, far from ruling

---

95   For different readings of Rousseau, see Arthur M.
      Melzer, "Rousseau and the Modern Cult of Sincerity,"
      The Harvard Review of Philosophy (Spring 1995): 4-21;
      Benjamin Storey, "Self-Knowledge and Sociability in the
      Thought of Rousseau," *Perspectives on Political Science*
      41/3 (2012): 146-54.

out the possibility of authentic sincerity, inauthentic forms of sincerity live, like parasites, off the experience of episodes of authentic sincerity. Like sincerity between friends, moreover, authentic sincerity is integral to living authentically. Both sincerity and authenticity are desirable, not simply in this or that instance, but throughout a life as a fundamental part of its orientation. In other words, personal identity and by extension authenticity (being true to that identity) are not fully completed states but ongoing, more or less habituated processes directed at ideals. We say that someone is sincere or that she is authentic, not because she is so unfailingly, but because she behaves for the most part in ways that show a settled tendency of striving to be sincere and authentic. Contrary to what the foregoing modern narrative might suggest, sincerity and authenticity are, at best, aspirations constitutive of a person's character yet never completely fulfilled or finished as long as a person has a breath left. They are modes of excelling in living that are repeatedly tested, exposed to elements putting them on trial. In short, sincerity and authenticity, being true to others and being true to ourselves, are virtues – and they are not particularly novel to modernity.

The virtue of being true to ourselves is already a staple of Aristotle's and Aquinas' accounts of the virtue of magnanimity. It is, however, particularly Aquinas' astute pairing of magnanimity with humility that outlines the necessary means of contending with the love of others' praise as the primary challenge to being authentic. As described below, his pairing of magnanimity and humility entails authentic sincerity, the deliberate attempt to be truthful. His treatment of this twin virtue demonstrates that sincerity and authenticity not only do not have to come apart, as the historical narrative of modernity has been read to suggest, but that there are good reasons to think that they should not.

Any review of Aquinas' account of magnanimity must begin, as he does, with Aristotle's portrait of the magnanimous person as someone who "thinks himself worthy of great things and is truly worthy of them" (*Nicomachean Ethics*, 1123b1-2).[96] Of all

---

96   For conciseness, I pass over significant discussions of magnanimity in the *Eudemian Ethics*, the *Rhetoric*, and the *Posterior Analytics* as well as its relation to a nameless virtue that, in contrast to magnanimity, is concerned with small honors (*NE* 1125b1-25). For discussion of problems associated with interpreting Aristotle's accounts, see René Gauthier, *Magnanimité: L'idéal de la grandeur dans la philosophie païenne et dans la théologie chrétienne* (Paris: J. Vrin, 1951); William F. R. Hardie, *Aristotle's Ethical Theory* (Oxford at the Clarendon Press, 1968), 119-23 and "'Magnanimity' in Aristotle's Ethics," *Phronesis* 23/1 (1978): 63-79; Howard J. Curzer, "Aristotle's Much Maligned Megalopsychos," *Australian Journal of Philosophy* , 69 (1991): 131-51; Michael Pakaluk, "The Meaning of Aristotelian Magnanimity," *Oxford Studies in Ancient Philosophy* 26 (2004): 241-75. In researching for this essay, I found particularly helpful Tobias Hoffmann's splendid essay: "Albert the Great and Thomas Aquinas

the things external to human beings that matter to
them, honor is the greatest; it is the greatest external good. A magnanimous person is accordingly
someone who has the right sort of disposition towards honor (*NE* 1123b21-22: περὶ τιμὰς δὴ
καὶ ἀτιμίας ὁ μεγαλόψυχός ἐστιν ὡς δεῖ).
That disposition is not so much a concern for hon-
or as such. After all, Aristotle observes, "there can be
no honor worthy of complete virtue" (*NE* 1124a8)
and a magnanimous person "counts honor for little,"
which is why he seems arrogant or at least disdainful (καταφρονητικός) for the sorts of honors that
others can confer (*NE* 1124a19). Being disposed towards honor in the appropriate way consists instead
in having an accurate sense of one's deservedness or
worthiness (ἄξιος) of honor (what is generally understood by a person's 'honorableness') and behaving
accordingly. A magnanimous person, in other words,
considers herself worthy of honor without striving
to be honored; she does not care about being honored because she knows that any honors she might
receive are incommensurable with her virtuousness,
what makes her deserving of honor. In sum, magnanimity is the settled disposition of managing the
pleasure taken in being honored and the ensuing
concern or desire for honor. It is the settled disposition of managing these emotions in the right way,

---

on Magnanimity" in *Virtue Ethics in the Middle Ages:
Commentaries on Aristotle's Ethics (1200–1500)*, ed. István
Bejczy (Leiden: Brill, 2008), 101-29.

such that a person cognizant of her honorableness esteems it neither too much nor too little.

Like any virtue, magnanimity is produced through a process by which practical reason repeatedly guides an emotion – in this case, presumably the desire for pleasure that accompanies the recognition of being worthy of honor – in an appropriate, moderating manner. In the case of magnanimity, practical reason provides that guidance by presenting the person with a true estimate of her worth, steering a path between overestimating herself (pride) and underestimating herself (pusillanimity).[97] The Aristotelian virtue of magnanimity is, in short, the virtue concerned with being authentic, with being true to ourselves in the sense of our true worth, regardless of what others – or, more precisely, what some others – think of us.

Two further aspects of Aristotle's account are relevant for our purposes here. First, magnanimity goes hand-in-hand with excelling in each of the virtues,

---

97   This crucial element of truth in magnanimity brings it close, as Irwin notes, to the settled disposition of someone truthful (ὁ ἀληθευτικός, ὁ φιλαλήθης) in word and life; *NE* 1127b2-3: "someone who is truthful both in what he says and in how he lives, when nothing about justice is at stake, simply because that is his state of character." Aristotle, *Nicomachean Ethics*, 2nd edition, translated with introduction, notes, and glossary by Terence Irwin (Indianapolis/Cambridge: Hackett, 1999), 220.

the task of a lifetime (*NE* 1123b30).[98] There is, in other words, no magnanimity "without complete virtue," and all-around virtuousness is what separates a magnanimous person from imitators, i.e., those arrogant individuals who consider themselves worthy of honor and superior to others solely because of their fortune, superior social position, riches, or power (*NE* 1124a29-b5). If there is ever a virtue that entails the unity of the virtues, it is magnanimity. Aristotle in fact deems it the crowning virtue, the jewel (κόσμος) of the virtues, because it both makes them greater and does not come about without them (*NE* 1124a2-3: μείζους γὰρ αὐτὰς ποιεῖ, καὶ οὐ γίνεται ἄνευ ἐκείνων).[99] But for that very rea-

---

98   Opinions differ on what this sentence entails. Pakaluk argues that the greatness of the great-souled individual encompasses all the virtues, but not greatness in each virtue; see Pakaluk, 258f.

99   This line gives rise to questions about (a) the nature of the augmentation and (b) the status of the virtue. Regarding (a), how can appropriate self-esteem make a person more courageous? Regarding (b), since magnanimity supposes that a person is virtuous in general, i.e., presupposes possession of particular virtues, it is not immediately clear how it can augment them. Answers to both questions may lie in the complexity of human motivation and reciprocity among the virtues, such that just as there is no magnanimity without courage and temperance, so there is no courage or temperance without magnanimity. We rightly think ourselves worthy of esteem, to be sure, because we manage our fears and

son, i.e., because it is not possible without a certain noble goodness (ἄνευ καλοκαγαθίας), Aristotle adds that it is truly difficult (χαλεπόν) to be magnanimous (*NE* 1124a3-4). This last remark reminds us that magnanimity, like any virtue, is fundamentally aspirational, something never perfectly achieved. As a settled disposition that results from repeatedly bringing practical reason to bear on our emotions (the part of our soul that is receptive to it), success in the past does not guarantee success in the future, as new situations call out new complexities of emotions.

A second feature of Aristotle's account pertinent to our concerns is his view of the magnanimous person's concern for truth and, we might add, her sincerity in relations with others. According to Aristotle, a magnanimous person is necessarily open, i.e., she makes no secret of the objects of her affection and she is no less forthcoming about who or what she hates. He adds that truth necessarily matters more to her than does someone's opinion and that she speaks and acts openly (φανερῶς) (*NE* 1124b27-29). From this emphasis on being open, i.e., on not hiding one's feelings but being truthful to others about them, it follows that Aristotle regards sincerity as part of magnanimity (which in turn, as argued above, is integral to being authentic).

---

desires for pleasures in the right way, but the reverse is no less true. For a discussion of these issues as the backdrop to medieval treatments, see Hoffmann, 102-06.

However, he adds a crucial caveat in this connection. The caveat stipulates a limit to the openness by way of explaining the motivation for it. She limits her candor when it comes to speaking to "the many" (πρὸς τοὺς πολλούς); when addressing them, she uses irony (εἰρωνεία) (*NE* 1124b30-31).[100] This remark comes on the heels of a comment about the difference between the magnanimous person's display of herself to the high and mighty and to ordinary folk. To the former she does not hide her greatness, to the latter she does, since "it is as vulgar in relation to inferiors [ἐν δὲ τοῖς ταπεινοῖς φορτικόν] as it is in relation to the weak to make a show of one's strength" (*NE* 1124b22-23).

Some of Aristotle's observations about the magnanimous (e.g., their idleness, slowness to act, a deep voice, measured utterances, a fondness for the aesthetic over the utilitarian) may be simply reports about how they are perceived.[101] As such, they are arguably not essential to being magnanimous. What is unclear is how the contingent and essential features are to be distinguished, specifically when it

---

100   Gauthier suggests that Aristotle has Socrates in mind here; René A. Gauthier et Jean Yves Jolif, *L'Éthique à Nicomaque*, Tome II: Commentaire (Louvain-la-neuve: Éditions Peeters, 2002), 283f, 290f, 293.

101   As Irwin and others suggest, his use of 'seem' (δοκεῖ) in this connection is his way of flagging that he is merely registering traits customarily associated with magnanimity; Irwin, 220, 222f.

comes to questions of how the magnanimous relate to others and how sincerely they conduct themselves in relation to some of them. In every society, to be sure, there are differences in social status and importance, and his remarks about the magnanimous person's relation to individuals from different social strata may be consistent with her having a true estimate of her worth, based upon her virtue alone. Nonetheless, Aristotle attributes to the magnanimous person a clear sense of her superiority. The attribution is particularly evident in his comparison of magnanimous persons with their imitators. After noting that the latter reproduce the former's disdain for others, Aristotle observes that someone magnanimous "is rightfully disdainful" (δικαίως καταφρονεῖ) (*NE* 1124b5-6). This sense of superiority explains her reticence to receive benefits, to remember what she has received, or to ask for help (since doing so, in each case, allegedly betrays inferiority). So, too, it explains the different ways that she relates to those who are and who are not – in her view or others' views – her inferiors, whether that inferiority is based upon social position or virtue.[102]

---

102   This disjunction is meant to leave open the difficult question of the extent to which these considerations bleed into one another. One might try to salvage Aristotle's account (from a Judeo-Christian perspective) by insisting that those who are deemed lesser or inferior in this connection are such only from the point of view of their virtue. But this interpretation has to reckon with

Aristotle insists, to be sure, that the magnanimous person's opinions about her virtue and about others are true. Yet, as noted above, she is less than sincere with others who are regarded as inferior. At least from a contemporary perspective, Aristotle seems to waver between characterizing magnanimity strictly as a virtue and characterizing it in terms of social status. In any case, although virtue and not fortune is the genuine basis of the magnanimous person's deservedness of honor and her understanding of her deservedness, it comes with a sense of superiority over specific others. In sum, because of her virtue, the magnanimous person is worthy of great honors and thereby superior to others – and cognizant of that superiority.

***

Prima facie at least, these features of Aristotle's account of magnanimity (notably, the less than fully sincere, ironic approach shown to some people, the sense of superiority) conflict not only with Judeo-Christian beliefs but also with modern egalitarian ideals. His account also seems to collide with the fact that an honorable person is invariably beholden to realities and powers beyond her for the features and capacities that make her deserving of honor.

Aristotle's explicit appeal to others' social positions in establishing the conduct of magnanimous persons. For how Aquinas might address similar issues, see n. 106 below.

Aquinas is, nevertheless, intent on appropriating Aristotle's account of magnanimity, and he responds to the difficulty of doing so by pairing his conception of magnanimity with humility.[103] Difficult as the prospects for this pairing might seem, it is further complicated by the fact that Aquinas construes magnanimity as a part of fortitude, and humility a part of temperance. This complication is no doubt due, at least in part, to the distinctive historical context (shaped by Stoic, Neo-Platonic, and earlier Christian sources) in which Aquinas addresses these issues.[104]

Despite these complications, Aquinas remains faithful to Aristotle's basic view that honor takes precedence over all external human goods and that a magnanimous person strives to do things that are worthy of great honor (*magno honore digna*), things that are "great simply and absolutely" (*magna simpliciter et absolute*), with little concern for honors as such.[105] Her concern, in other words, is not to

---

103   *Summa theologiae* II.II, q. 161, 1.

104   *Summa theologiae* II.II, q. 129, 5; q. 161, 4. At the time that Aristotle's texts became available to Aquinas, the discussion of virtues had already been couched in Stoic and Neo-Platonic terms. For discussion of indirect as well as direct sources on which Aquinas draws, see Gauthier, *Magnanimité*, 296-465, and Hoffmann, 101-29.

105   *Summa theologiae* II.II, q. 129, 1, q. 129, 1 ad 3; q. 129, 2; q. 129, 3; *Opera omnia* 10: 58; *Scriptum super libros in Sententiarum magistri Petri Lombardi Episcopi Parisiensis,*

be feared or loved by others, but to be deserving of
the same. Nonetheless, the honors are great honors
(as they are for Aristotle), of the sort facilitated by
fortune.[106] In Aquinas' terminology, honors are the
matter proper (*materia propria*) to magnanimity (the
"special good" that makes it a "special virtue"), but
they are not the end.[107]

In the characterization of this end, Aquinas' modification of Aristotle's account starts to become
apparent. The end of magnanimity is to carry out

---

ed. P. F. Mandonnet (vols. 1-2) and M. F. Moos (vols.
3-4) (Paris: Lethielleux, 1924-47) II.42.2.4, 2.

106   According to Aquinas, honor is the greatest external
good since it is (a) closest to virtue, existing as a testament
to the latter; (b) accorded to God and the best things; and
(c) pursued above all other things. Following Aristotle,
he also notes an unnamed virtue concerned in parallel
fashion with "ordinary" honors; see *Summa theologiae* II.II,
q. 129, articles 1-3 and 8. The fact that not everyone is in a
position to perform acts worthy of great honor presents a
problem for the accessibility of the unity of the virtues as
Aristotle conceives them. Hoffmann identifies two solu-
tions – one Aristotelian, one non-Aristotelian – offered
by Aquinas, where the Aristotelian solution consists in
developing the proper potential (*potentia propinqua*) for
the exercise of the magnanimity, should fortune provide
a person with the wherewithal; see Hoffmann, 121-24.

107   *Summa theologiae* II.II, q. 129, 8: "...magnanimitas
ad duo respicit, ad honorem quidem sicut ad materiam;
sed ad aliquid magnum operandum sicut ad finem." See,
too, II.II, q. 129, 2 and q. 129, 4; Hoffmann, 119-21.

something great that is supposed to be done (*aliquid magnum operandum*). Whereas each virtue respectively indicates something that is supposed to be done, magnanimity aims at doing it as well as possible and thereby perfecting the virtues as a whole. A person is deserving of honor to the extent that she perfects the virtues, the excellences of character, and doing so is equivalent (not identical) to being magnanimous. Hence, a magnanimous person is indifferent to external goods (presumably honors themselves), valuing them only to the extent that she considers them useful to perform acts of virtue.[108] So, too, she is neither impressed by great honors, "since she considers herself above them," nor broken by being dishonored (*dehonorationibus non frangitur*), since she recognizes that the like is done to her "undeservedly" (*indigne*).[109]

One might contend that Aquinas here is simply tweaking Aristotle's description of magnanimity.[110] Perhaps, yet Hoffmann points out that Aquinas shifts

---

108   *Summa theologiae* II.II, q. 129, 7 ad 1 and ad 2.

109   *Summa theologiae* II.II, q. 129, 2, ad 3; q. 129, 7 ad 3.

110   Lindsay Cleveland, "A Defense of Aristotelian Magnanimity against the Pride Objection with the Help of Aquinas" in *Dispositions, Habits, and Virtues*, Proceedings of the American Catholic Philosophical Association, 88 (2015): 259-71. Cleveland contends that the essential features of Aristotelian magnanimity do not entail the pride exhibited by the Aristotelian magnanimous person (ibid., 262).

the center of gravity somewhat from Aristotle's account. Whereas magnanimity for Aristotle is a mean
for a worthy person's self-esteem simply, Aquinas ties
that self-esteem to its import for good actions. Someone is magnanimous "who esteems himself worthy of
great things, that is, so that he may do great things
and have them done to him should he indeed be worthy."[111] So, too, Aquinas alone seems to be insisting
that a lack of magnanimity is a moral failing.[112]

In any case, Aquinas's characterization of magnanimity as a part of fortitude represents a clear departure from Aristotle's conception, even if the gloss on
fortitude bears Aristotle's imprint as well. A person
with fortitude (courage) is able to withstand and
combat grave dangers appropriately; she manages to
remove impediments to doing the right (reasonable)
thing, impediments that principally take the form
of fears. In other words, with her eye firmly on the
prize, i.e., a good proposed by reason, she manages

---

111   *Sententia libri Ethicorum* (*Opera omnia* 47), 4. I, p.
       226: "ille videtur esse magnanimous qui dignum se ipsum
       aestimat magnis, id est ut magna faciat et magna ei fiant,
       cum tamen sit dignus." Hoffmann, 120f.

112   *Summa theologiae* II.II, q. 130, 1; *NE* 1125a19;
       Hoffmann, 121. Yet while what Aristotle deems a vice is
       not the same as what Aquinas considers a sin, Hoffmann's
       claim that Aristotle sees in puffed-up persons "merely a
       cognitive, not a moral defect" seems to overreach (ibid.).

to suppress those fears and confront mortal dangers steadfastly, even aggressively.[113]

Like fortitude, magnanimity strengthens the soul with respect to something arduous by struggling with passions that resist reason. Whereas fortitude struggles with passions whose strength is in some sense internal to them, i.e., passions of excessive fear or daring, magnanimity contends with passions whose force derives from the objects of the passions. Echoing Augustine in this regard, Aquinas speaks of the "love or craving" (*amor vel cupiditas*) of honor and praise. We fail to be magnanimous when, succumbing to this craving, we hope for, and imagine ourselves deserving of, more or less than the honors we deserve. As Aquinas puts it, what fear is to fortitude, hope is to magnanimity. Yet, just as virtue in general consists in safeguarding "the good of reason" in human affairs, and fortitude in particular does so in the face of grave dangers, so magnanimity is a virtue be-

---

113   *Summa theologiae* II.II, q. 123, articles 2-6. Aquinas distinguishes fortitude in a broad sense (the "firmness of mind" required by any virtue to act "firmly and immovably") from this special virtue of fortitude (*Summa theologiae* II.II. q.123, articles 1, 2, and 4). By treating magnanimity as a part of fortitude in the latter sense, Aquinas follows, often by his own lights, a tradition that includes Chrysippus, Cicero, Macrobius, Philip the Chancellor, and Andronicus (see *Summa theologiae* II.II, qq. 128-29).

cause it does so in regard to great honors.[114] Employing the nomenclature of his day, Aquinas concludes that magnanimity is a quasi-integral and potential part of the special virtue of fortitude: "quasi-integral" because, unlike the latter, it confronts fears involved in pursuing what it takes to be worthy of great honors, not the fear that a grave danger like death presents[115]; "potential" because magnanimity, while not

---

114   *Summa theologiae* II.II, q. 129, articles 2, 3, 5, and 7. In other words, magnanimity, as the settled disposition to pursue difficult excellences that are deserving of honor, is a part of fortitude; to be in the habit of denying this pursuit would be "small of us," the very antithesis of magnanimity, as would be the habit of thinking ourselves "bigger than life," as delusions of grandeur shape our desires.

115   As Aquinas puts it, only someone magnanimous in a certain sense is ready to expose himself to danger for the sake of something great (*Summa theologiae* II.II, q. 129, art. 5, ad 2). What prepares the soul for the endurance and aggressiveness required by fortitude is what Cicero in *De inventione rhetorica*, ii, 163 calls 'confidence' (*fidentia* for which Aquinas writes *fiducia*), "through which the soul itself embarks on great and honorable things with a sure hope and trust in itself" (*per quam magnis et honestis in rebus multum ipse animus in se fiduciae certa cum spe conlocavit* (www.thelatinlibrary.com/cicero/inventionae2.shtml)). Citing Aristotle in the main response to the question, Aquinas observes that "magnanimity seems to be the same as confidence, about great honors" (*Summa theologiae* II.II, q. 128, 1). This remark, however, is not Aquinas' last word on the subject, as he notes Macrobius' emendation of Cicero's list of the parts of fortitude, an

the whole power of fortitude, nonetheless brings it to bear on a secondary matter.[116] It is a distinct virtue, "secondary" to fortitude as the "principal" virtue, in the two senses that roughly correspond to being a quasi-integral and potential part of it.[117] Having extended our desires to great things, magnanimity

---

emendation that singles out magnanimity and security, "which Cicero includes under confidence." Aquinas notes Macrobius' modification approvingly, since, while confidence is a hope for great things, hope "presupposes" (*praesupponit*) desire for the things hoped for and magnanimity is precisely "the appetite extended to great things through desire" (*Summa theologiae* II.II, q. 128, 1 ad 6). Thus, while confidence concerns the certitude of hope, magnanimity concerns the magnitude of both what is hoped for and the desire for it; Macrobius Ambrosius Theodosius, *Commentarii in Somnium Scipionis*, 1.8.7, ed. James Willis (Leipzig: Teubner, 1963), 38; William Harris Stahl (trans.), *Macrobius: Commentary on the Dream of Scipio* (New York: Columbia University Press, 1952¹, revised edition, 1966).

116   Aquinas differentiates three kinds of parts: subjective (ox and lion as parts of animal), integral (wall and roof as parts of a house) and potential (nutritive and sensitive powers of the soul); see *Summa theologiae* II.II, q. 48. Fortitude has only "quasi-integral" and "potential" parts. The notion of a quasi-integral part is found in the anonymous, Stoic-oriented compilation *Moralium dogma philosophorum*, ed. John Holmerg, and adopted in Philip the Chancellor's *Summa de bono*, ed. Nikolaus Wicki (Bern, 1985), 806, 823f.

117   *Summa theologiae* II. II, q. 129, 5.

is the Ciceronian confidence, the faith and hope in ourselves that we must have to embark on them.[118]

Earlier I noted how Aquinas modifies Aristotle's conception of magnanimity by stressing the pre-eminent place of the disposition to perfect the virtues as one of the great things pursued (the deservedness of honor). Aquinas' treatment of magnanimity as a form of fortitude represents a further departure, at the very least from the letter of Aristotle's account. But the difference between Aquinas' and Aristotle's conceptions of this virtue becomes even starker when we turn to the way Aquinas builds humility into a single virtue that also comprises magnanimity.

Given the sense of superiority that Aristotle builds into the virtue of magnanimity, its difference from humility seems obvious. To his credit, Aquinas directly confronts this issue, citing Aristotle's apparent claim to that effect, while also noting that Aristotle does not include humility among the virtues.[119]

---

118   *Summa theologiae* II.II, q. 129, 6. Confidence is a robust sort of hope, arising from some consideration that provides a firm belief (*vehementem opinionem*) of obtaining some good. Precisely insofar as it is this sort of hope, linked to some grounded and thus firm belief of achieving some good, confidence "pertains" to magnanimity. Thus, there is no magnanimity without desire for a particular good and a confidence (i.e., reasonable hope) of attaining it.

119   *Summa theologiae* II.II., q. 161, 1, obj. 5. Ross translates the small-souled (μικρόψυχος) as "unduly humble" (*NE* 1123b10) in *The Complete Works of*

His first step in this regard is to demonstrate that magnanimity and humility are not contraries. That demonstration begins with the observation that in human beings we find great things (gifts from God) as well as defects inherent to the human condition. A person is magnanimous if consideration of those gifts leads her to deem herself worthy of great things; she is humble if consideration of her shortcomings leads her to give little weight to herself (*parvipendat*). These considerations, though made by the same person, are patently different. Hence, Aquinas concludes, magnanimity and humility are not contraries, though they seem to pull in different directions "because they proceed according to diverse considerations."[120]

Yet, far from being content with demonstrating the non-contrariety of magnanimity and humility, Aquinas wants to show their complementarity and mutual necessity. His first move in this direction is to note the different sorts of attitudes produced by pursuit of an "arduous good." The goodness of this end – i.e., the fact that there is a good reason (*rationem boni*) for it – makes it attractive, prompting hopes and dreams for it. The difficulty of obtaining it, however, has the opposite effect, prompting res-

---

Aristotle, ed. Jonathan Barnes, Vol. Two (Princeton, New Jersey: Princeton University Press, 1995), 1773. So, too, Grosseteste uses *humiles* to translate "lowly people" in Aristotle's account; see Hoffmann, 115.

120   *Summa theologiae* II.II, q. 129, 3 ad 4; q. 161, 1 ad 3.

ignation and despair. In other words, we experience
hope if the good appears attainable, despair if not.
From the fact that the nature of the good affects us in
both ways at once (hoping for it and despairing of it),
Aquinas infers the need for a twofold virtue (*duplex
virtus*), comprising one moral virtue "that tempers
and restrains the soul, lest it tend immoderately to
lofty things [*excelsa*]....[and] another that strengthens the soul against despair and impels it to the pursuit of great things in keeping with right reason."[121] It
would be a mistake to hope for too much, as it would
be to despair, to hope for too little; humility restrains
the former hope, magnanimity counters the latter.

Aquinas does not provide much in the way of clar-
ification of his use of *duplex* in this connection, but
he apparently considers magnanimity and humility
distinct virtues, with distinct rationales.[122] He refers

---

121   *Summa theologiae* II.II, q. 161, 1: "Una quidem quae
temperet et refrenet animum, ne immoderate tendat in
excelsa, et hoc pertinet ad virtutem humilitatis. Alia vero
quae firmat animum contra desperationem, et impellit
ipsum ad prosecutionem magnorum secundum rationem
rectam, et haec est magnanimitas."

122   The reason for being magnanimous, for strengthening
the soul against despair, is that it is necessary to attain
the good proper to the soul; by contrast, the reason
for humility is reverence for God and what it entails,
namely, that a person "not ascribe more to herself than is
appropriate to her in keeping with the position [*gradum*]
allotted her by God" (*Summa theologiae* II.II, q. 161, 2).
Though Aquinas does not explain the sense of *duplex* in

to humility as a moral virtue, and does the same for magnanimity. Yet their complementarity and mutual necessity follow from the fact that they respectively manage emotions concerned with the same thing, the same arduous good, and do so as dictated by reason.[123] Whereas magnanimity (as a part of fortitude) gives us the courage to pursue great things within reason, humility (as a part of temperance) has the moderating effect of curbing our tendencies to pursue them excessively (beyond our capacities). Any pursuit of great things on our part requires both magnanimity and humility – the former to fortify us against acquiescence and defeatism, the latter to counter "presumptuous hopes" and "excessive self-confidence."[124]

In order to avoid being carried away into things beyond her (*feratur in ea quae sunt supra se*), a person needs to know her deficiencies.[125] This knowledge helps her regulate her inclinations and desires, "so that she does not esteem herself beyond what she is."[126] Indeed, in contrast to pride, "humility attends

---

the phrase *duplex virtus*, one likely source is Cicero's *De inventione rhetorica*.

123   *Summa theologiae* II.II, q. 161, 1 ad 3: "Ad tertium dicendum quod humilitas reprimit appetitum, ne tendat in magna praeter rationem rectam. Magnanimitas autem animum ad magna impellit secundum rationem rectam."

124   *Summa theologiae* II.II, q. 161, 2 ad 3; q. 161, 4 ad 3.

125   *Summa theologiae* II.II, q. 161, 2.

126   *Summa theologiae* II.II, q. 161, 6.

to the rule of right reason, according to which someone has a true estimate of oneself."[127] Aquinas takes
pains in this connection to spell out the relation
between humility and the relevant knowledge, i.e.,
the knowledge that takes the form of a rule guiding
a person's appetite for great things and the honors
they bring. While supposing this knowledge, humility is not the knowledge, the true estimate of oneself
as such. "Instead humility essentially consists in the
appetite itself."[128] Humility is a person's settled disposition of modifying her inclinations ("presumptuous hope") and making choices, both in keeping with
what is reasonable. This last qualification obviously
cannot mean that a person who possesses humility
must have a perfectly true estimate of herself. But
it does mean a practice of abiding by a reasonable
rule, i.e., a rule mostly likely to provide a person with
some measure of a true estimate of her capacities. In
this way, Aquinas is simply reinforcing the basic contention that humility is a virtue – neither an emotion nor desire, neither an act nor a decision (though
it touches, as a virtue, on all of the latter).[129]

---

127   *Summa theologiae* II.II, q. 162, 3 ad 2: "...humilitas
attendit ad regulam rationis rectae, secundum quam
aliquis veram aestimationem de se habet."

128   *Summa theologiae* II.II, q. 161, 2.

129   Since humility requires a true estimate of oneself,
it cannot be a form of self-deception or involve a denial
of one's abilities (gifts). The appearance of such a denial,
individuals' putative obliviousness to their humility, and

For Aristotle, too, as noted above, the magnanimous person has a true estimate of herself, albeit an estimate that includes an awareness of her deservedness of honors and superiority to most other people. By contrast, one of the effects of a humble person's true estimate of herself is that she "laudably casts herself down to the lowest places."[130] This self-projection (more precisely, a *deiectio*) displays, not self-contempt *tout court*, but contempt for one's moral failings and contriteness in the face of them. When a person has the virtue of humility, she is in the habit of attempting to secure a true estimate of herself (one that neither overestimates nor underestimates her qualities), but with the regret of not being able to do so unfailingly. With humility comes a sense of remorse in the face of our failings along with the understanding that a lifetime of virtue can never completely eradicate the inclinations responsible for them. But, by the same token, humility provides a powerful foundation for gratitude – at odds with elements of Aristotle's portrait of magnanimity.

---

so-called "paradoxes of humility" have led contemporary authors to argue that humility is in fact a "virtue of ignorance"; see Julia Driver, "The Virtues of Ignorance," *The Journal of Philosophy* 86/7 (1989): 373-384. Yet, while the argument faithfully reports certain uses of 'humility' and 'modesty,' those uses neither exemplify nor disestablish humility as a virtue in the Aristotelian sense.

130   *Summa theologiae* II.II, q. 161, 1 ad 2.

The contrast with Aristotelian magnanimity is sharpened further by the different conceptions of relationships to others. To be sure, a similarity exists as well. Just as the magnanimous person recognizes her superiority to most other people, so humility entails an awareness of capacities – literally, "what is of God in herself" (*id quod est Dei in seipso*) – that are not subject to the authority of others.[131] Nonetheless, Aquinas adds, since reverence is owed to what is from God in everyone, "we ought, through humility, to subject ourselves to all our neighbors for God's sake."[132]

Herein lies a salient part of the reason for thinking that magnanimity and humility make up a twofold virtue. Humility puts the brakes on presumptiveness, the aspiration to be superior to others who are, in fact, our equals in God's eyes. Humility restrains a desire to make others in our own image, in effect, the image of what renders us feared or loved in their sight. By construing humility and magnanimity as one, Aquinas lays the groundwork for expanding the potential for magnanimity beyond confines conferred by a particular social status.[133] The fundamental feature of magnanimity, the settled disposition to esteem oneself appropriately, i.e., in keeping with one's deservedness of honors, remains. But the

---

131   *Summa theologiae* II.II, q. 161, 3.

132   *Summa theologiae* II.II, q. 161, 3 ad 1.

133   See note 106 above.

honors need not be the great honors paid to society's blue-bloods but the great honors deserved by everyone who lives a virtuous life. In this sense, sistered with humility, magnanimity becomes a virtue of liberal politics, not tied to a particular class or station, but spread equally across the entire community of God's children.

***

On the previous pages, I have tried to show how Aquinas modifies Aristotle's conception of magnanimity, boldly transforming it into a virtue that demands humility no less than a sense of one's honorableness. The fact that the twofold virtue elaborated by Aquinas is directly concerned with honors places it squarely in the context of the issues of identity and authenticity addressed throughout this essay. Those issues concerned challenges to being authentic (being true to ourselves) presented by controversies over the status of a person's identity, given the multiple sorts of identities (organic, embodied, and social) incorporated by it. The primary challenge to authenticity, I suggested, is what Augustine characterizes as the inordinate desire to be feared or loved by others, a desire that springs in no small part from insecurity about the very prospects of preserving oneself and one's personal identity. I introduced Aristotle's and Aquinas' accounts of magnanimity to dispute the popular view that authenticity in this sense is an exclusively modern moral concern. By way of concluding, I would like to make explicit some neglected but promising implications of Aquinas' account of this virtue for these issues.

The first implication is for the meaning of authenticity itself. Viewed as the virtue of being true to ourselves, being authentic requires us to be true to what is most essential to us, i.e., a distinctive potential to excel that each of us possesses as part of an unfinished personal identity (organic, embodied, and social) and the experience of it. To excel as a human being is, as both Aristotle and Aquinas stress, to be in the habit of striving to be honorable, worthy of esteem. To achieve this excellence, they also agree, is exceedingly difficult, given false hopes and presumptuous delusions, on the one hand, and unreasonable fears and despair in our abilities, on the other. Hence, being true to ourselves in this regard requires nothing less than a virtuous combination of magnanimity and humility. We would not be true to ourselves, were we to fasten single-mindedly on high-flying hopes, ignoring our reasonable fears, or let our fears smother our hopes. In other words, being authentic demands the virtue of humility to moderate our hopes so that we do not succumb, driven by insecurities, to the notion of being more deserving than we in fact are. But it also demands no less the virtue of magnanimity to embolden us, in face of our insecurities, to strive to do what is honorable, to accomplish what make us genuinely worthy of esteem.[134]

A further implication of Aquinas' account is the fragility of authenticity and its dependence on factors beyond ourselves. In order to come to a true estimate and esteem of ourselves, we need help – and not only in the form of good fortune. We also desperately need others to show us not only who we are and optimally can be but also the worthiness and, yes, the loveableness of being true to that reality and potential. Only with the help of others ("the communion of saints"), can we approach some measure of a true estimate of ourselves, an estimate that makes abundantly clear our neediness and dependence upon others as well as our genuine prospects for doing great things, the sort of things that confirm our honorableness. Appreciating that neediness, humility restrains the movement of any hope in ourselves alone, while magnanimity strengthens the resolve to pursue a life of virtue as our only authentic and thereby truly estimable aspiration.

I have been using the first person plural rather loosely just above, particularly when we recall that

---

134   Humility is a tempered self-esteem that coincides with the emboldened self-assurance characteristic of magnanimity. Humility is the instantiation of a human being's earthiness, the hiddenness of past and future ("from dust to dust") but also the present time-space, the place, however, on which magnanimity, the instantiation of a human being's worldliness, confidently builds.

Aquinas uses singular pronouns to characterize humility. But I do so deliberately, since humility restrains our hope in ourselves, both individually and collectively. Restraining this hope coincides with having a true estimate of our personal identities as embodied individuals, the social identities incorporated in those personal identities, and the identities of the societies in which we find ourselves. In corresponding ways, magnanimity gives us the strength to realize the potential for excellence that resides in those identities. Humility is matter of being true to the experience of our limitations, thrown into the world as we are, embodied in a distinctive time-space and utterly dependent upon it. Yet being true to that experience brings with it the promise of the possibilities for excellence that we project for ourselves in that same world. We find ourselves outfitted with a fragile but real potential to survive and perhaps flourish and excel, but only if we are true to this potential, i.e., only if – thanks to others and powers beyond our control – we have the greatness of soul to combat our fears of failing and reach out to what is reasonably within our reach.[135]

---

135   These remarks obviously provide no recipe for addressing pressing issues that fall under the broad banners of the climate, social justice, economic productivity, and the like. Yet in each case, policy-makers (i.e., all of us) have to confront concrete challenges of overestimating and underestimating our potential for addressing them.

Realizing our dependency on others is central to the virtue of humility, the virtue that, together with magnanimity, is the virtue of authenticity.[136] As noted above, Aquinas stresses that humility requires a degree of submissiveness to others, specifically, to what is from God in everyone else. This aspect of the virtue of humility contrasts sharply with the modern narrative that authenticity and sincerity come apart. Being authentic by way of the virtue of humility and magnanimity entails being honest about oneself, with oneself and others. This virtue is singularly at odds with any attempt to render one's words or behavior more attractive or beguiling than truthful. To be insincere is precisely to attempt to shape, even master how others regard us, to have them fear or love us rather than see us for what we are (and then love us accordingly).[137]

---

136   See Guignon, *On Being Authentic*, Chapter 8 and Somogy Varga, *Authenticity as an Ethical Ideal* (New York: Routledge, 2011).

137   The sincerity of honestly exposing ourselves to others at the risk of their rejection is obviously a necessary condition of loving and being loved – always *ohne Gewähr*. The meaning of this risk – to risk being authentically sincere while accepting that we are not in control – requires both the fortitude of true self-esteem and the tempering force of humility. In short, though there is no guarantee, there is no love without the twofold virtue of magnanimity and humility. As usual, the Bard puts it best: "This is the monstrosity in love, lady, that the will is infinite and the execution confined; that the desire is boundless, and

To be sure, the whole point of the fuss over Rameau's nephew (the advance it allegedly represents over Rousseau) was to illustrate a sincerity that is disturbing because it is authentic, someone who is sincerely amoral because he is authentic.[138] But note that authenticity here refers to who Rameau happens to be, divorced from who he can or should be. The modern narrative is right to argue that supposed sincerity without authenticity (read: the narrative's image of Rousseau) is insincere, but the narrative would have us believe that authenticity and the sincerity it entails (read: Rameau's nephew, Conrad's Kurtz) can only exist in a moral vacuum. We can follow Shakespeare's exhortation only if we take the plunge into the heart of darkness where there is no moral light.

But, like the figures that supposedly epitomize it, this position is pure fantasy. It disastrously overlooks how personal identity is a fusion of a person's embodied identity with her social identities, how that fusion permits obfuscation and deception only against the backdrop of truth and truthfulness, how language and other cultural accouterments are enabling no less than confining, how the means of being

---

the act a slave to limit." Thanks to Gary Riebe, SVD for bringing this line to my attention many moons ago.

138   Trilling uses this expression to characterize a belief of 19th century English novelists, but it applies to his and Williams' view of Rameau as well; Trilling 114f; Williams, 189.

insincere – as the negative prefix suggests – suppose the experience of sincerity. As mentioned earlier, the narrative also treats sincerity and authenticity alike as facts or permanent character traits rather than as virtues that embody settled but unfinished dispositions that can only be rendered intelligible and real by reference, not only to aspirations and ideals but to repeated tests of them.[139] Viewed through the lens of Aquinas' twofold virtue, Rameau's nephew and Conrad's Kurtz are both singularly lacking in humility and magnanimity. Their sincerity is inauthentic, precisely because they regard all social intercourse as a sham rather than as an inherent part of their lives, limiting in certain respects, liberating in others. Lacking humility, they refuse to accept those limitations; lacking magnanimity, they despair of exploiting that liberating, indeed, transformative promise of life with others.

Of course, matters are in reality far messier than this talk of the aspirational character of sincerity and authenticity in terms of magnanimity and humility might suggest. Because who we are and should be is not independent of our relationships, authenticity entails sincerity. But far from being a one-size-fits-all commodity, the character of sincerity is relative to the relationships involved. High levels of candor and openness go hand-in-hand with mutual trust

---

139   Augustine, Epistola XCV, 2 in *Patrologia Latina*, ed. J.-P. Migne, Vol. 33 (Paris: Garnier, 1845), 353: "Ecce unde vita humana super terram tota tenatio est."

between friends and intimates. But revealing oneself indiscriminately to others without a basis of trust can hardly be consistent with being true to ourselves (indeed, today it can be a recipe for "identity theft," an expression that, while overreaching, is not simply a euphemism). In other words, sincerity demands discretion.[140] This demand is patent in confidential relationships that restrict a person's freedom to reveal certain facts about the other person in the relationship. In some cases, violation of this confidentiality is in fact a crime; in other cases, it is simply a case of indiscretion.[141] Because being true to ourselves entails being true (faithful) to others to whom we have such a relationship, sincerity towards those outside the relationship must be discreet. In the best case, discretion enables us to maintain confidenti-

---

140   Instructive in this connection is the legal conception of discretion (the stepchild of Aristotle's ἐπιείκεια), the power or right to act in certain circumstances based upon one's own judgment. Judicial discretion in matters of equity, not strictly covered by the letter of the law, and police discretion in determining what violations to enforce are analogous.

141   Criminal violations of confidentiality can involve relationships between doctor and patient, lawyer and client. Non-criminal but no less egregious violations range from betrayals of secrets between lovers or friends to betrayal of the trust in a priest hearing a confession.

ality, to keep from revealing secrets, without being dishonest, i.e., insincere towards others.[142]

***

Being true to ourselves is, I have been arguing, a virtue, a virtue that is attainable but also ever-perfectible over the course of a life. As the virtue of thinking neither too little nor too much of ourselves, authenticity requires both magnanimity and humility, fortifying but also tempering our confidence in ourselves. In the first part of my remarks I contended that modern speculative challenges to the idea of personal identity present no threat to this virtue since those challenges suppose impoverished views of human experience that cut it off from a person's organic identity. So, too, in the second part of my remarks, I argued that practical challenges to the integrity of personal identity, given its social formation, gain traction only by ignoring the role played by individuals with their own personal identities in the dynamics of social processes and their ability –

---

142 Aquinas addresses this issue when he defends the magnanimous person's use of *ironia*, not the sin opposed to truth (*ironiae mendacium*), but a person's practice of acknowledging her negatives without showing "her entire greatness" (*Summa theologiae*, II. II, q. 113, 1 and II.II, q. 129, 3 ad 5). It should be noted that the sin consists, by contrast, precisely in feigning some negatives about oneself (*minora de se fingit*) (*Summa theologiae*, II.II, q. 113, 3 obj 1).

as part of the process of shaping their own personal identities – to subject those social processes, not least internalized forms of those processes, to rational evaluation.

That same capacity for rational evaluation, a responsiveness to the truth, is the key to the existential challenge to authenticity. This final and primary challenge arises from a desire, driven by an all-too-human fundamental insecurity, for others' respect and affection, displayed in the form of praise and honor. Our best hope and chief means of responding to this challenge and accepting Shakespeare's exhortation is to develop the virtue of being authentic, being honest with ourselves about who we are and can be. If I am right, the 'virtue of authenticity' is not only a new name for an old virtue, but a virtue that we can begin to understand by returning to the wisdom of Aristotle and Aquinas.

The Aquinas Lectures
Published by the Marquette University Press
Milwaukee WI 53201-1881 USA
http://www.mu.edu/mupress/

1. *St. Thomas and the Life of Learning.* John F. McCormick, S.J. (1937) ISBN 0-87462-101-1

2. *St. Thomas and the Gentiles.* Mortimer J. Adler (1938) ISBN 0-87462-102-X

3. *St. Thomas and the Greeks.* Anton C. Pegis (1939) ISBN 0-87462-103-8

4. *The Nature and Functions of Authority.* Yves Simon (1940) ISBN 0-87462-104-6

5. *St. Thomas and Analogy.* Gerald B. Phelan (1941) ISBN 0-87462-105-4

6. *St. Thomas and the Problem of Evil.* Jacques Maritain (1942) ISBN 0-87462-106-2

7. *Humanism and Theology.* Werner Jaeger (1943) ISBN 0-87462-107-0

8. *The Nature and Origins of Scientism.* John Wellmuth (1944) ISBN 0-87462-108-9

9. *Cicero in the Courtroom of St. Thomas Aquinas.* E.K. Rand (1945) ISBN 0-87462-109-7

10. *St. Thomas and Epistemology.* Louis-Marie Regis, O.P. (1946) ISBN 0-87462-110-0

11. *St. Thomas and the Greek Moralists.* Vernon J.Bourke (1947) ISBN 0-87462-111-9

12. *History of Philosophy and Philosophical Education.* Étienne Gilson (1947) ISBN 0-87462-112-7

13. *The Natural Desire for God.* William R.O'Connor (1948) ISBN 0-87462-113-5

14. *St. Thomas and the World State.* Robert M. Hutchins (1949) ISBN 0-87462-114-3

15. *Method in Metaphysics.* Robert J. Henle, S.J. (1950) ISBN 0-87462-115-1

16. *Wisdom and Love in St. Thomas Aquinas.* Étienne Gilson (1951) ISBN 0-87462-116-X

17. *The Good in Existential Metaphysics.* Elizabeth G. Salmon (1952) ISBN 0-87462-117-8

18. *St. Thomas and the Object of Geometry.* Vincent E. Smith
    (1953) ISBN 0-87462-118-6
19. *Realism And Nominalism Revisited.* Henry Veatch (1954)
    ISBN 0-87462-119-4
20. *Imprudence in St. Thomas Aquinas.* Charles J. O'Neil (1955)
    ISBN 0-87462-120-8
21. *The Truth That Frees.* Gerard Smith, S.J. (1956)
    ISBN 0-87462-121-6
22. *St. Thomas and the Future of Metaphysics.* Joseph Owens,
    C.Ss.R. (1957) ISBN 0-87462-122-4
23. *Thomas and the Physics of 1958: A Confrontation.* Henry
    Margenau (1958) ISBN 0-87462-123-2
24. *Metaphysics and Ideology.* Wm. Oliver Martin (1959)
    ISBN 0-87462-124-0
25. *Language, Truth and Poetry.* Victor M. Hamm (1960)
    ISBN 0-87462-125-9
26. *Metaphysics and Historicity.* Emil L. Fackenheim (1961)
    ISBN 0-87462-126-7
27. *The Lure of Wisdom.* James D. Collins (1962)
    ISBN 0-87462-127-5
28. *Religion and Art.* Paul Weiss (1963)
    ISBN 0-87462-128-3
29. *St. Thomas and Philosophy.* Anton C. Pegis (1964)
    ISBN 0-87462-129-1
30. *The University in Process.* John O. Riedl (1965)
    ISBN 0-87462-130-5
31. *The Pragmatic Meaning of God.* Robert O. Johann (1966)
    ISBN 0-87462-131-3
32. *Religion and Empiricism.* John E. Smith (1967)
    ISBN 0-87462-132-1
33. *The Subject.* Bernard Lonergan, S.J. (1968)
    ISBN 0-87462-133-X
34. *Beyond Trinity.* Bernard J. Cooke (1969) ISBN 0-87462-134-8
35. *Ideas and Concepts.* Julius R. Weinberg (1970)
    ISBN 0-87462-135-6
36. *Reason and Faith Revisited.* Francis H. Parker (1971)
    ISBN 0-87462-136-4
37. *Psyche and Cerebrum.* John N. Findlay (1972)
    ISBN 0-87462-137-2

58. *Metaphysics and Culture.* Louis Dupré (1994)
    ISBN 0-87462-161-5

59. *Mediæval Reactions to the Encounters between Faith and Reason.*
    John F. Wippel (1995) ISBN 0-87462-162-3

60. *Paradoxes of Time in Saint Augustine.* Roland J. Teske, S.J.
    (1996) ISBN 0-87462-163-1

61. *Simplicity As Evidence of Truth.* Richard Swinburne (1997)
    ISBN 0-87462-164-X

62. *Science, Religion and Authority: Lessons from the Galileo Affair.*
    Richard J. Blackwell (1998) ISBN 0-87462-165-8

63. *What Sort of Human Nature? Medieval Philosophy and the
    Systematics of Christology.* Marilyn McCord Adams (1999)
    ISBN 0-87462-166-6

64. *On Inoculating Moral Philosophy against God.* John M. Rist
    (2000) ISBN 0-87462-167-X.

65. *A Sensible Metaphysical Realism.* William P. Alston (2001)
    ISBN 0-87462-168-2.

66. *Eschatological Themes in Medieval Jewish Philosophy.* Arthur
    Hyman (2002) ISBN 0-87462-169-0

67. *Old Wine in New Skins.* Jorge J. E. Gracia (2003)
    ISBN 0-87462-170-4.

68. *The Metamorphoses of Phenomenological Reduction.* Jacques
    Taminiaux (2004) ISBN 0-87462-171-2.

69. *Common Sense: A New Look at an Old Philosophical Tradi-
    tion.* Nicholas Rescher (2005) ISBN-10: 0-87462-172-0;
    ISBN-13:978-0-87462-172-3.

70. *Five Metaphysical Paradoxes.* Howard P. Kainz (2006)
    ISBN: 0-87462-173-9; ISBN-13: 978-0-87462-173-0.

71. *St. Thomas and Form as Something Divine in Things.* Lawrence
    Dewan, OP (2007) ISBN 978-0-87462-174-7.

72. *Aristotle's Divine Intellect.* Myles F. Burnyeat (2008)
    ISBN 978-0-87462-175-4.

73. *What Happens after Pascal's Wager: Living Faith and Rational
    Belief.* Daniel Garber (2009) ISBN 978-0-87462-176-1.

74. *What Is Reparative Justice?* Margaret Urban Walker (2010)
    ISBN 978-0-87462-177-8.

75. *Perception as a Capacity for Knowledge.* John McDowell (2011)
    ISBN 978-0-80462-178-5.

77. *Omnisubjectivity: A Defense of a Divine Attribute*. Linda Zagzebski (2013). ISBN 978-0-87462-183-9.
78. *Moral Sprouts and Natural Teleologies 21st Century Moral Psychology Meets Classical Chinese Philosophy*. Owen Flanagan (2014). ISBN 978-0-87462-185-3.
79. *The Story of My Life: Narrative and Self-Understanding*. Richard Moran(2015). ISBN 978-0-87462-187-7
80. *The God of the Bible and the God of the Philosophers*. Eleonore Stump (2016). ISBN 978-0-87462-189-1
81. *Identity, Authenticity, and Humility*. Daniel O. Dahlstrom (2017). ISBN 978-0-87462-191-4

About the Aquinas Lecture Series

The Annual St. Thomas Aquinas Lecture Series began at Marquette University in the spring of 1937. Ideal for classroom use, library additions, or private collections, the Aquinas Lecture Series has received international acceptance by scholars, universities, and libraries. Hardbound in maroon cloth with gold stamped covers. Uniform style. Some reprints with soft covers. Complete set (ISBN 0-87462-150-X) receives a 40% discount. New standing orders receive a 30% discount. Regular reprinting keeps all volumes available. Ordering information (purchase orders, checks, and major credit cards accepted):

Marquette University Press
Phone: (800) 247-6553
or order online at: http://www.mu.edu/mupress/

Editorial Address:
Dr. Andrew Tallon, Director
Marquette University Press
P.O. Box 3141
Milwaukee WI 53201-3141
Tel: (414) 288-1564 FAX: (414) 288-7813
email: andrew.tallon@marquette.edu

www.marquette.edu/mupress/

ISBN-13: 978-0-87462-191-4
ISBN-10: 0-87462-191-7

$15.00